Maybe you feel defeated or simply distraught in this modern world of degenerate insanity. Many of us maintain a docile decorum whilst living in a comfortable trance of relative normalcy. We allow ourselves to be sedated by the latest gadgets, and programmed by the decadent influences of Hollywood. These distractions keep us pacified, demoralized and reluctant to pursue a life of true nobility.

Awaken

This is my story
I left a world of comfortable complacency
Entered the realm of the living
On a quest
To analyze my beliefs
Discover my inner truth

They say we need a revolution
I say we need a R E V E L A T I O N

Question everything you understand to be true
Relentlessly examine established ideas
Meticulously challenge ingrained dogma
Test theories using praxis
Take back your power and awaken the warrior spirit

Arise

Perhaps you are ready to wake up. Perhaps you are ready to face the great delusion. Only by virtuous revolt will we stand a chance at combating this modern moral decay. The ideas, stories, and life experiments in this book are meant to enliven the warrior within—to awaken a dormant desire to live with greatness, dignity and honor. Perhaps my story, my struggles, can aid you in the battle for sovereignty.

RETURN YOUR REVOLT INTO **V I R T U E**

REVELATION
A RETURN TO VIRTUE

First published in the United States of America

Published in 2015

ISBN: 978-0-9861726-0-1

Printed in the United States of America

Set in Optima

Cover design by Regina Marsh

Cover art by Kimberly Diamandopol

Jayme Louis Liardi is a Long Island native and a graduate of Stony Brook University with a degree in Environmental Humanities and Theatre Arts. While Revelation: A Return to Virtue is his first venture as an author, Jayme plans to further develop his vision and refine the ideas expressed in this book. You can reach him at: jayme.liardi@gmail.com or through his website: jaymeliardi.com

For

June A Liardi
Who gave me
Life
Opportunity
Love

and

Louis J Liardi
Who taught me
Conviction
Courage
Confidence

I owe everything to you

My deepest gratitude

To my brothers
who taught me how to fight

To my mentors
whose wisdom I heed
courage I carry
vision I bear

To the masters
the warriors
those that came before me
whose heroism is my inspiration

REVELATION

A RETURN TO VIRTUE

JAYME LOUIS LIARDI

CONTENTS

REVOLT AGAINST THE MODERN WORLD

.I.
YOUTH

.II.
DISCOVERY

RETURN YOUR REVOLT INTO **VIRTUE**

.III.
PRAXIS

.IV.
AWAKENING

FOREWORD

by

Marc Fasanella, PhD

The dawn of the 21st century is a perplexing time to be alive. In the "civilized" world, we are overwhelmed with information (often conflicting) that purports to inform us what we must know in order to be educated, productive and reasonably healthy citizens. Many of us tune out the babble that tries to tell us what to eat, what to wear, where to live, and how to earn in order to thrive. What is presented to us as the pinnacle of attainment seems calculated to be a bit beyond our reach, anyway. Those of us who see ourselves as progressive pursue the only perceived option and strive to do the least possible harm to ourselves and to others. We exercise when we can, try to eat healthily, live as simply as life's complexities allow, and stay out of debt until an illness or a holiday sets us back. For the most part, we follow the herd around us, struggle to keep up with the necessities of daily life in the technology-oriented, wage and credit based, consumer culture that has become the snare of modern life. It is hard for us to imagine any other way to live, to

envision other strategies to cope with our
existence. Keenly aware of the creature comforts we
enjoy, we muddle through—live day to day, week to
week, paycheck to paycheck, alternating between
frenzied work, boredom, complete exhaustion, and
ecstatic celebration. Not sure where we'll end up—the
forecast we hear informs us that our savings,
investments and retirement aren't all that secure, our
health will fail, our brains degrade—it sometimes
seems hopeless, even dystopic. A not-too-distant
dystopia is in fact the future most often portrayed in
television and film. If we look outside of our "civilized"
existence, much of the developing world is at war—
living a nightmare that creates millions of casualties,
orphans, rape victims and refugees each year as they
struggle to have the relative security and standard of
living we have.

And then you meet someone like Jayme. He is all
inquiry, personal experiment, living life by his
ideals. His tenacious questioning of the veracity of the
status quo, ability to radically alter the circumstances of
his life, and insistence on envisioning aspects of a more
utopian existence, is disarmingly fresh. What he
proposes in this book would do much to ensure a life
of economic simplicity, personal health, and mental
clarity for each of us. With an engaging sense of
wonder, charmingly humorous outlook, and knack for
storytelling, Jayme communicates his insight, and
inspires and empowers us to reflect on our notion of
ourselves, our way of life, our plans for our

future. Reading REVELATION: A Return To Virtue, is an uplifting lesson on reflection and praxis shared through a personal journey. This book proclaims, challenges, motivates, and models. It is an important contribution to a swelling tide of independent thinking that just might lift humanity out of the muck and mire of a dispiriting age of delusional commerce.

PROLOGUE

*'Twenty years from now you will be more disappointed by
the things that you didn't do than by the ones you did do,
so throw off the bowlines, sail away from the safe harbor,
catch the trade winds in your sails.
Explore, Dream, Discover.'*
Mark Twain

January 2013

I am talking to my half-naked self in the middle of a rural road in Keaau Hawaii. I am exuberant now that the sun has come out in this jungle, and for whatever reason I decide to talk to myself. I begin to ask myself questions like 'what do you want in life?' and 'what makes you unique?' I spend two hours wandering the gravel roads talking to myself, working out the pent-up frustrations of a desire that has been building since childhood—the desire to make an impact in this world is surfacing and I am riding the wave. Just as the surfer places all his faith in the wave, knowing that if he just follows its path of motion he will be successful; I too, am riding my own wave, and it is exhilarating.

How did I get here?
How did I get to be working on a farm in the heart of the rainforests of Hawaii?
How did I go from couch potato 12 year old to 100-mile-bike-ride completing athlete at 22?
How did I go from shy self-conscious kid to confident and motivated young man?

As I work through the whirl in my head, I learn about the things I don't want in my life, the kind of lifestyle that I wish to avoid. Through this exercise, I am able to discern what I love on the most basic levels—pursuing truth, improving my life and the lives of those around me, motivating others, and making them laugh and smile. It is this moment that is one of the pivotal turning points in my life. I am becoming conscious of my true self.

Arise

The purpose of this book is to strengthen you. It is a tool that will help inspire you to take that essential action that we are all so afraid of taking. So many of us travel through life rushing to get nowhere—a race to nowhere. I think of what my life would have been like if I had chosen this path, if I had chosen the path now commonly traveled upon in the developed world.

I would have probably chosen a major in college that would get me a "good job" and apply to grad school in a field that would pay well and let me retire early so I could then live my life. I would probably have started getting antsy around age 28 and realize that most people my age were getting married so I would, in haste, get married to whomever I was with. We would have had 2.5 kids (the national average), a dog named Lucky, a suburban house with a plastic fence near good schools. I would have worked this "good job" until age 65, when I could finally live the life I had always wanted, or the life I was told to want; but all the while, throughout these years, I would have had this deep emptiness inside—a feeling of self-repression. I would have wondered what my life would have been like if I had just done the "not safe" thing, if I would have just followed my bliss and remained loyal to my heart.

But, for many of us, the choices that we make in life for our future, the decisions that shape our entire lives, are not our own decisions! These ideas of the "perfect" or "normal" life are ideas placed into our heads by the culture we find ourselves enveloped in, the default programming experienced by us all during our youth. Through a combination of media and school, we are led to believe that this is the only choice we have—that it is either this or you're alone and homeless. Through fear we buy into this story and develop lives that are not fully ours and wonder why we feel disgruntled and hollow. Our minds have been commandeered, and it's time for us to take them back.

The good news is that you picked up this book: the good news is that you have the power to change your situation this very moment. The life experiments, stories and overall vision contained within, will empower you to make the changes and take the necessary steps in your life to attain the true freedom that you desire and innately deserve.

I made a choice in the jungle of Hawaii, under the light of the new sun, that I was not going to go down the ordinary route, that I was going to follow my heart to the end and see how deep my main roots run. This book is the story of how I got to this point, through what seemed like endless adversity. I share with you my hopes and dreams, in the hope that they will inspire you to actualize your dreams, no matter the cost.

Awaken

REVOLT AGAINST THE MODERN WORLD

.I.
YOUTH

IMAGE

'Do not go where the path may lead; go instead where there is no path and leave a trail.'
Ralph Waldo Emerson

My imagination as a kid was wild and crazy: like most kids I was always being something or someone different and always exploring the possibilities of my imagination. I was experiencing other worlds on a visceral level while still being grounded in this reality. Somewhere along the way, I lost this sense of wonder.

I don't know where it went, but it seemed to have vanished by the time I was 11 years old; I was no longer preoccupied with experiencing a newly discovered tree at a friend's house, but instead wanted to reach the next level on the PlayStation.

Why did my imagination, my sense of wonder, leave me at such a young age?

At the time I had no idea, and I did not even question: what I did was take the path of least resistance—or so I thought at the time.

I decided that if I wanted to fit in, I would need to do as I was told: I would need to become a part of the team and follow the crowd.

In preschool, when I was four years old, the teacher and I quickly became close. This was not due to any kind of great teacher-student relationship, but because (on more than one occasion) I would lead the others into the room with all of the toys—this was, of course, against the rules.

Like the leader of a three foot mob, me and the other kids would storm into the play room because that's what we wanted to do—we wanted to play; we didn't want to sit around and listen to someone telling us what we need to do, what we need to learn, and what we need to think about.

As you can probably imagine, I was on the bench (the impromptu jailhouse reserved for four year old rascals) most of my preschool career. This was my first experience with authority beyond my parents, and I was finding it difficult to resist the chains that seemed to be creeping onto my body without my authorization.

I disliked this feeling of oppression.

Fast forward to second grade—I am seven years old and I am in love with the most beautiful girl in the class. Despite her not knowing this, I am confident that she will reciprocate my complete love and we will live happily ever after.

I am determined to let her know how much I feel for her, so I decide to write 'Dear Alexa, I love you. Let's get married!' on a piece of construction paper and give it to her at the end of the school day.

I go and give her the paper, and she looks at it, then up

at me, and starts laughing, thinking that it's just some joke. Once she realizes, from the look of horror and rejection on my face, that it is not a joke, she gets up and tries to console me, but I run straight for the bathroom. I cry my eyes out—I feel a pain that I never want to feel again.

As I cry in the bathroom, my friends knock on the door to let me know that it's time to leave, that the buses are arriving soon. I didn't care, because in that moment, I felt as if nothing else mattered but the pain.

I continued my school career, gradually slipping away from my natural state of play and blissful freedom—my effortless way of existence and learning—and into a place of unwarranted control, a state of constant fear of judgment and of negative repercussions. As a student, I learned that in order to make it through the system unscathed I would need to acquiesce and yield to the rules of the system—I would need to play the game.

So that's what I did.
I played the game.

I made sure that I was always "paying attention" to the teacher, which just meant looking at them and raising your hand once in a while. I also made sure I never questioned what they were saying, because once you do that, you become regarded as a problem and as someone who needs more discipline.

Despite my rising need to liberate myself from the indoctrination station, I opted to play it cool and be the good student; my rationale was that as soon as I reached my senior year in high school I would defect from this false sense of security and move back into my true identity. What I failed to realize was that this new way of seeing, acting, and viewing the world that I had bought into would become my reality.

I had become an agent for a system I so earnestly wanted to escape. I was going through the motions of the "typical" person in my stage of life.

Go to school
Reject authority telling you what to do
Question teachers
Get in trouble in class
Get reprimanded
Learn to be submissive
Be a good student
Get good grades
Make the honor role
Pacify the mind with TV, movies, video games, drugs or alcohol
Join as many clubs as you can
Be the president of as many clubs as you can (it looks good on your résumé)
Follow your dreams
But be realistic
Participate in extracurricular activities
Have an internship
Learn to drive
Get a part-time job
Learn the value of hard work
Pacify the mind with TV, movies, video games, drugs or alcohol
Follow your dreams
But be realistic
Apply to colleges

Write essay entailing why you are worthy
Like a slave waiting upon a benevolent master
Get into a "good" college
Graduate high school
Go to college
Say to yourself, 'I'm going to recreate myself'
But the recreation looks strikingly similar to the old version
Feel guilty for not living up to your own standards
Pacify the mind with TV, movies, video games, drugs or alcohol
Realize newfound freedom
Drink a lot of alcohol
Meet a lot of people
Get in trouble in class
Question professors
Begin to question college
Begin to question thoughts
Begin to question the future
Have the feeling that you've been living a lie
Begin to see through the illusion
Question your beliefs, habits, diet, lifestyle, reality
Begin anew

MUSIC SEX & GAMES

*'The only way to deal with an unfree world is to become
so absolutely free that your very existence is an act of
rebellion.'*

Albert Camus

I realized early on, like most people, that being forced
to do things only made me angry and resentful. I
realized that when I was forced to study math, read a
book, play an instrument, my desire left faster than you
could say the word "homework." Throughout
elementary and middle school, I resented teachers
because they were the ones forcing me to do all this
nonsense that I didn't want to do. It was pointless to
me, and all I wanted to do was play outside and look at
bugs and climb trees. Why couldn't I do that? What
made learning about Columbus and his adventure in
1492 so important?

I would go through days forgetting all the "important"
facts that I needed to learn and instead dream of what
life was like outside the oppressive walls of grade
school. I found that the only times I enjoyed were those
spent in gym and recess. These places were *free,* I
didn't have my parents or my teachers telling me what I
could or couldn't do—it was time I could spend being
me. I quickly learned that the best way for me to be
happy was to ensure my freedom.

Whenever there was a homework assignment, I would
always do it my way and defy the instructions. If there

was a group project, I would find a way to "hack" the directions and create the best available route for the team. I would go out of my way to complete it in the way I saw fit, despite whatever repercussions followed, which would often be in the form of a scolding or grade deduction.

I didn't care.

I was expressing my freedom in the only way I could at the time. But more importantly, I was doing what I felt was right: I was making the best of seemingly repressive and oppressive circumstances and turning them into an opportunity for creativity and problem-solving.

This approach continued throughout middle school and early high school; I quickly began to see that my unconventional style was being met with increasing pressure from the administration. My teachers began to require more cookie-cutter type answers and gave less freedom of expression. I began to feel restricted, like an animal being slowly cornered. It was then that I discovered music and its ability to evoke feelings of freedom and limitless expression.

This was exciting. Prior to this, my experience with creating music had always left a bitter taste, because it was something that was forced on me as a kid. At the age of ten, I was required to choose an instrument to play for the next eight years of school. I was given the privilege of playing the cello, and at first I wrestled with the notion of being forced to play an instrument, but then I accepted the fact and wanted to do the best I could. So I played in the school orchestra and practiced my scales, all the while being interested in being the best I could be. Years went by and I came to develop a talent for the instrument; I received awards for my playing at various competitions—but I felt unfulfilled: it seemed as though it was all for nothing, a shallow victory. I now realize that I didn't accomplish those things for me, or for the joy of the journey: I simply did what I was told, what was required as a good student and a good musician. I was becoming a person I did not want to be. I was becoming domesticated! I did not enjoy this feeling. I felt cheated, as though all my work was in vain.

So I quit.
I began anew.

I loved music for the innate freedom of expression it brought me, but my structured experience with it left me questioning not only the school system but my own intentions. At the time I was enveloped in this thought, the choir director of the high school came into our orchestra rehearsal telling us the benefits of singing for our ear's ability to distinguish pitch. I knew I enjoyed singing as a kid, so I jumped at the opportunity, hoping to find what I was searching for.

Singing allowed me to tap into a power I had forgotten I was capable of expressing. When singing with various a Capella groups, I was allowed the opportunity to express myself, to have fun with my voice and creative energy—something I had been lacking prior to this discovery.

But it wasn't enough. I still felt unsatisfied, trapped in a cage and I didn't know why. Throughout high school, I found myself getting lost in the creative world of video games and becoming increasingly introspective.

Despite not feeling powerful, I felt in control of my own world through video games. There came a point where I spent the majority of my free time in my bedroom in front of the television screen with a controller in my hands.

My life became a predictable cycle of events:

Go to school
The movies
The mall
Play video games
Eat fast food
Repeat

A path that was becoming less and less fulfilling for me.

***

In elementary school, I had an ability to know who the "weakling" was in the class, the kid who just couldn't seem to fit in with anyone. I would spot them almost instantly and, more often than not, make friends with them as soon as I was able. This ability was noticed by my teachers, and on more than one occasion I was asked by teachers to make friends with the new kid or with the kid who was being made fun of. The teacher would talk to me in private, discussing how important it is to make other kids feel important and welcome, I gladly accepted the request every time. I enjoyed the feeling it produced: the simple act of making other people happy and changing their view of the world around them left me with a sense of belonging and importance. Eventually this gift of mine would be swept under the rug and replaced with the more "important" things taught in the classroom (mathematics, spelling, geography, etc.) and would go underdeveloped for many years, in the shadow of trivial factoids and relentless memorization.

I felt like I was losing oxygen, choking up, facing problems while having to dance for various teachers, working through my frustration with society, government, pollution, the opposite sex, my family, my body, everything that seemed to be conspiring against me.

No longer
Will I make an excuse
Play the victim
Blame someone else
Be a slave to my perceived limitations
Stop the flow of my creativity
No longer will I not be me

All of these seemingly small events culminated to reach
a critical point, a level of intensity which would lead
me to question the very path I found myself walking. I
knew that this path, worn by many who have traveled
its repressive way, with its seductive comforts and
fictitious security, was not suited for me and the person
I knew I was destined to be. I yearned for the rapture
that an authentic adventure could bring. If I were to
remain on this path, I would be effectively marching
slowly to my own demise, for the luxuries and comforts
that would placate my physical being would not
extinguish the anguish my spirit would quietly endure.

It was time to reroute.

I had no idea where I was headed, let alone how to get
there: the only thing I knew for certain was where I
didn't want to end up. This was all I needed to set my
life on fire, to begin a new adventure, to discover
exactly what I was capable of, to journey within and
perform the self-work needed to make an impact in the
world I knew I was destined to make.

Some friends thought I was downright mad for wanting
something more than a good job, a comfortable living,
and a cozy couch to collapse on after a long day's grind

in monotony. I didn't care: just like in the jungles of Hawaii, a fire had been lit deep inside my being and it was not going to be extinguished. I felt the warmth of wonderment.

I began to seek those that were getting results, the people that were making the changes that I wanted to make. Once on this path, I found myself realigning my life. I formed new creeds, discarded burdensome belief systems, and began to lose friends, lose contact with family members. I found myself walking a path alone most of the time.

A lone wolf on the hunt of a lifetime

Despite my newfound conviction, I remained encased in the confines of an educational system of indoctrination and found it difficult to follow this newfound inner truth while submerged in a sea of conformity and complacency.

'It takes courage to grow up and turn out to be who you really are.'
E.E Cummings

INDOCTRINATION

'I have never let my schooling interfere with my education.'

Mark Twain

It wasn't easy deciding to follow my heart. I doubted myself and questioned whether my dream was worth chasing. But these moments don't last long, for nothing can suppress the ardor of our spirit, once invigorated.

Going through the schooling process, which I call the "indoctrination of fear program," you start to become numb to your heart's true desires as you get shuffled into preexisting boxes to be shipped out into the *real world*.

We go to a set building for learning called a school, and in this big box are smaller boxes for the different categories called "classes" or "subjects"; there is a math box, a science box, an art box, a music box, an English box, a history box, etc. In these boxes, we learn highly specific, compartmentalized types of information. We call this information "knowledge." We go from one box to the next, trying to gain knowledge so we can get to the next set of boxes, i.e. grade level. We do this for years, hopeful that we will get into a prestigious university where we can really focus on the box we like the most. We get into university and work hard at attaining as much information about this one particular box as possible in the hopes that we will graduate from this grand box we call university with a piece of paper called a diploma that is supposed to signify our achievement in mastering The Boxes. But what we fail to see is that by viewing everything in boxes, we miss the magnificent truth that is the interconnectedness of everything. With "box" thinking, we no longer see things for what they are, and we train our children to think in this myopic way. We've strayed away from the ideal of the "Renaissance Man" that was so revered during the height of the Renaissance to the contemporary zeitgeist that praises specificity and specialized thinking. We maintain this narrow-minded view of the world and then teach it to our children; we teach them to see the world myopically, and with their vision impaired they stumble through life in our path.

Placing kids in straight rows and teaching them to sit still and be quiet is not a coincidence.

Schools were first created as a way of getting children off of the streets and helping to prepare them for the world. It's not that those who designed the school system were malevolent and out to squash the dreams of children, they were just being *realistic,* and in being realistic they were working to provide a workforce that would fit the context of the times. You see, back then, industry was booming, which meant that there were countless factories springing up that needed obedient, docile workers to run the various machines and perform duties in the industrial plants. We as a society quickly realized that if we created a workforce that was desirable before the workers began working in the factories, we would get a head start and become more prosperous as a nation. Well, our plan worked. It worked extremely well: we had more than enough young people who were capable of performing menial jobs in the factories. The kinds of people we needed to "produce" as a society were those who were compliant, who would respect and fear authority, be obedient, follow instructions, not think outside the box, never question things, and remain loyal. This type of education was highly desirable and valued because it allowed the country to carry out what it wanted to— which was the Industrial Revolution at the turn of the century. What I am trying to say is that this kind of education is not inherently "evil"; it's just what society thought was right at the time. We needed to have the right kinds of people for the kinds of jobs available to the public. Of course, not everyone became a factory worker; if you were one of the fortunate sons who came from a wealthy clan, you were sent to a private school that allowed you to philosophize, to travel and to experience the richness of life so that you would use your inherited wealth and newly acquired wisdom for the betterment of mankind.

Well, times have changed and we now see how broken this system is. We can see that if we want to grow as a society, if we want to create the world of our dreams, we need to first recognize the problem. When fear is used as the primary force by educators to motivate youth along the conveyer belt, creativity and passion are inevitably destroyed (or at least severely diminished). There is simply no wiggle room, no leeway, no possibility for those who want to go slower or faster, those who do things differently or experience things on a different level.

Let's look at the student who is fascinated by tigers for example. The child who is passionate about tigers does not need anyone to tell him he needs to learn about tigers: he just learns it out of an eagerness, because he *loves* tigers! He will come into class knowing the history of tigers, his favorite breeds, what they eat, where they live, anything and everything will be embraced and he will be proud of his "work." You absolutely cannot get this same level of work ethic from a child that is told to do a research paper on the same subject—it cannot be done. The only way to get those who are not passionate about something to feign passion is by fear, it is by telling students they will be graded, tested and quizzed and that they'd better do their best ... or else!

We are training students to have the skills of the late 19th century workforce, and we wonder why the economy is in recession. We tell our kids to follow their dreams, but then we unmaliciously crush them in a school system that teaches them to be "realistic."

Somehow, with our schooling system, we have destroyed that eager desire for education, for pursuing topics and ideas that we find interesting. Imagine how many of us have not read a book that could potentially change our lives just because of the process of indoctrination. When we equate learning, when we equate reading a book, with being tested, with being judged and graded, many of us may begin to loathe books and learning and stop partaking in the process altogether. Looking back to the days of Da Vinci, Machiavelli, and many others, it was customary that scientists, musicians, painters, sculptors, inventors, poets, would find their passion and then a mentor who was successful doing what they wanted to do, and then learn and cultivate their craft alongside their selected counselor. Why is it that today we choose to beat these various topics into everyone's head until they develop a passion? We have moved away from a society that allows people to find and cultivate their talents and dreams, to a system that creates citizens who perform well on tests, who are able to listen to instructions. This approach is regressive and counter-productive: there has to be a more efficient and elegant way of creating successful, well-learned citizens.

Learning is a *choice:* it isn't something that is done to you.

More schooling is not the solution. Our governments are pouring *billions* of dollars into a sixteen-year education system. You would think that we would want to make the most efficient use of this money when there is a sixteen-year investment; not to mention that this investment will impact the coming generation of the economy and culture. What we need to realize is that a problem cannot be solved on the level of consciousness in which it was created.

We need to see the root cause of the disease if we have any chance of healing and preventing the disease from spreading. Socrates said, 'the unexamined life is not worth living.'

So, why is this important? Today we continue living life the *same* way with the *same* institutions and leadership, and wonder why we don't see changes occur.

Our schooling system is a perverse and archaic system that needs a complete overhaul to go with the changing

times. We no longer have the stimulus of the late 1800s
or the context of the factories of yesteryear. We have a
new context, one which requires imaginative, intrepid,
and creative problem-solvers without a rulebook but
wielding a toolbox.

We need people
Who are able to see the whole picture
Able to see beyond the frame
Who don't need step-by-step instructions
Who are completely capable
Who are adaptable
Those who hunger for change

What we need is a system of schooling that allows
students to cultivate their own innermost passions: a
system that harbors and cultivates through trust and
magnanimity.

Let's replace indoctrination with cultivation.

CULTIVATION

*'Educating the mind without educating the heart is no
education at all.'*

Aristotle

In 1914, the multiple choice test was created and
implemented by a professor by the name of Frederick
Kelly. He designed the test for the sole purpose of
temporarily sorting an ever-expanding workforce into
the right slots; he did not intend for this test to become
the pernicious behemoth that it has become today. A
few years after the creation of the test, Professor Kelly
stated publicly that the test actually does more harm
than good and that it needs to be revoked as a measure
of intelligence and should only be used in a minute
number of instances. He was soon fired from his
position and the test was given more power in
academia.

The multiple choice test is just a symptom of a system
that is ailing, a system that is in need of a drastic
diagnosis and renovation. Instead of addressing
symptoms of this failing education system with ideas
such as the "no child left behind" program or the "race
to the top" initiative, let's look at the root cause.

Let me be clear that those who set up our education
system were not bad individuals or out to destroy the
creative human spirit; they were merely reacting to the
needs of the society at the time. Well, that is precisely
what we are doing: we are addressing the needs of

society today, and this requires a complete overhaul of our education system to create something that is in line with a sustainable and dignified civilization.

What is the purpose of school, anyway? If we are going to talk about a solution, we need to address *why* we need a formal education system for our children. The purpose of school is to create people who will support and sustain a healthy civilization. The current system seeks the lowest cost, stifles creativity, and promotes uniformity while rewarding mediocrity. We can see that this is destroying our economic prosperity and innovation; it is homogenizing our culture and setting a low bar for entertainment that lacks depth and integrity.

We can do better than this!

Learning is a *choice*: it isn't something you can force into the mind of someone using fear. We are creative, intelligent, and invigorated—must we accept mediocrity as the pinnacle of our ingenuity? We are hard-wired to want to commit to something grander than ourselves, and our brains thrive in this feeling of importance, of the feeling that *we* matter, that *we* can make a difference. The current Indoctrination process, however, does the opposite of this; it works to keep students from following their dreams and cultivating their creativity.

OK, OK, schooling is failing us, but what can we do about it? It's too big to *revolutionize*, isn't it better to just make small improvements that will one day create something we are proud of?

This is the thinking that we have had during the last few decades. More money, different teacher training, fewer field trips, more testing, different testing, reworked curriculum—all of these things are just bandages, tiny fixes trying to solve a problem that needs a more drastic solution.

But let's get to the basics.

There are four main reasons for having a formal education system:

1: Creating an organized and well-coordinated group of people we call a society

2: Having members of the society be well informed

3: Cultivating and guiding the pursuit of knowledge for knowledge's sake

4: Understanding the past and effectively applying the lessons learned from history

If we focus on these core principles of education, we will inevitably craft a society of skilled, compassionate citizens willing and able to create the reality needed for the times. When we focus on these core concepts and aim to form complete individuals, we create a well-functioning economy and society as a byproduct, because the citizenry are fully realized, impassioned and creative people. The raw material used is of the highest quality, therefore the end product is going to be of the highest quality as well.

It's the law of cause and effect—what you reap is what you sow.

We currently tell our students and our children to follow their dreams, but our actions would indicate otherwise. Our actions tell them to find "realistic" jobs, to follow their dreams only when the time is right, and that they need security first. All of this is well-intended, but it does not matter how sincere our hearts are if the underlying system that supports us is disingenuous.

So I propose a new paradigm: a paradigm that allows us to mean it when we say, 'follow your dreams.'

Let us teach our students

To question dogma
The importance of dignity
The principle of self-reliance
To take initiative and remain steadfast
To be open, honest, transparent and why it matters
To cultivate their innate talents and gifts
To relentlessly pursue truth
To deal with criticism
To overcome fear

Let's have a policy of open book/notes 100% of the time. Why would we ignore the fact that we have the Internet and force students to memorize when we could put that energy into creativity and discovery? It is time for us to recognize the absurdity of the multiple choice test, and testing in general. Let us evaluate students' progress by the level of experience they gain from specific tasks and projects. This is a much more accurate and dignifying way of evaluation. By doing this, we don't use the fear of a bad mark on a test as the driving force for learning; we use the students' own passion, their own fervor, as the motivating influence for an authentic education.

Why not have cooperation be the lifeblood of the students instead of having competition be the force driving the classroom? We are naturally creative, intelligent, and able to make superior decisions in the calm environment of cooperation than in one of anxious competition—we are social creatures, meant to work together. When two or more minds come together with a common goal or interest, the outcome is far greater than the sum of each person's capabilities.

Let's have individualized teaching that teaches to the student and not the test. Actually, we can do better than that: why not have teachers that teach *with* students—teachers that work with each student on a personal basis. The teacher will then be a guide, a coach, a mentor for the student to cultivate their own learning process. We are already doing this in some places, and we see an incomparable difference to those taught in the conventional way. We know how to do it, it's just a matter of how to make this approach commonplace.

We know what to do
How to change the situation
Make it superior
It starts with revelation

It's a question of desire
How desperately do we want this?
The moment we realize that *we* have the power
Is the moment our world changes

Realize your greatness
Rise and behold your brilliance!

.II.
DISCOVERY

THE MYSTERY MEAT

'The creation of a thousand forests is in one acorn.'
Ralph Waldo Emerson

It is my first semester of college, freshman year, and I am enthusiastic for the new possibilities. I am excited to question my belief systems, to find out what I'm capable of, and who I am. It is my second night in the dormitories, and our entire floor (around 25 of us) decides to head over to the dining hall to eat dinner. I go to get what to me is dinner food—a plate of meat with some vegetables.

I wait patiently as the woman serving the food places this rectangular black object on my plate alongside a modest portion of roasted potatoes. I get back to where the group is seated and I notice that they all have variations of the same dish—mystery meat coupled with some sort of vegetable.

I can still smell it, the foul, oppressive odor of the mystery meat.

In that moment I ask myself 'why the hell am I eating this? It doesn't smell good, it looks like a charred brick, and I bet it tastes just as awful as it looks!'

As I am thinking this, I begin to bring my thoughts out into the open air and let my newfound friends in on my inner dialogue. I begin to ask them why, why would we be eating this if it so obviously is not appetizing to us.

One person, who I would later know as Chris, said, 'Dude, stop thinking about it so much, it's food, just eat it.'

But this comment only fueled my fire and I exclaimed, 'Why are we going against our instincts and eating this garbage? I'm not saying I'm a vegetarian by any stretch but I don't think we should just blindly accept this as "food." What does this say in a broader sense? Should we just blindly accept the habits and ideas instilled upon us by society or our families? What does that say about us, if we are willing to blindly go with whatever dogma is most common in our society at the current time?"

Well, you could probably imagine how popular I was at this point. More than half of the group got up and left due to my existential crisis and the questioning of our collective eating habits.

The remaining six of us began to discern why we were blindly deciding that this food was worth eating without even thinking that an alternative would be possible. We were eager soldiers with a burning desire to take back our minds from the malevolent clutches of dogmatic belief.

***

11:50pm

I am lying on my bed in my dorm room with my three friends and decide that it would be a great idea to hug and kiss the leg of one of them as a joke. This is me drunk for the first time. I decide that despite my preconceived notion that drinking isn't for me, I will try it out. I mean, how bad could it be?

I, my roommate Felix, and another friend of ours, Leo, decided to go to The American Boychoir concert (yes we are full-fledged music geeks). After the concert, we stopped by the dining hall to eat. Felix said to me, 'Come on, J! You need to get out of your little shell and drink with us sometime. You don't have to get drunk, but you should really get out more. Life is about experiencing different things, even if you don't like them.'

I smiled and wondered why I had been making the choices in my life up until this point—why I had been playing it safe. I realized that my gut reaction was to go home that night and get to bed early like I usually did, but instead, I decided to do the opposite. So I called my friend Brian, who I knew would be having a party that night. It was a Thursday, and knowing Brian, since the day of the week ended in "day," we would be set with a place to go.

We headed over to his room and were still 10 feet away when Brian yelled, 'Well I'll be damned, J is that you?

I'm surprised you are still awake at this hour, isn't it passed your bedtime? Don't worry champ, I'll make sure you have a real good time!'

The voice inside my head told me that I should just head back home, but I decided to be comfortable in my own discomfort and ride the wave. Stepping inside the 12 by 19 foot space I was astonished by how many people were packed into this tiny room! I swear there must have been at least 13 people. Brian handed me a can of beer and told me to just 'chill and relax.'

As I tried to chill, I began to drink the beer—not too bad. I looked back for Felix and Leo and only saw Felix talking to someone else. I asked him where Leo went, and he told me that he left, that he doesn't like drugs and that he gets uncomfortable around booze. I couldn't help but feel a sense of guilt: 'Am I doing the "wrong" thing on purpose? Am I going against my intuition to broaden myself as a human being or am I just giving into the pressure from others and my own insecurities?'

As I was zoning out and having this inner dialogue I was startled by the voice of Brian: 'Dude, I've been trying to get your attention for two minutes, you want another beer? You drank that one pretty quickly for a newbie!' I nodded and decided that whatever would come would be a learning experience. I decided that I would be confident in the choices that I make, that I was fully responsible for my decisions and no one else.

The principle of self-reliance.

I smiled to myself and decide to talk to the others in the

room. We were having a great time, laughing, joking, and sharing each other's company. Before I knew it, I had downed two beers and two rum and cokes and was on my third! I was feeling the intoxicating effects and was just content with chuckling to myself in the corner as long as I had my friend Captain Morgan with me.

I realized at this point that everyone was leaving, so I decided to follow them. Brian told me that everyone was headed to a house party down the road and explained that this was just the opening event. I couldn't understand why someone would drink themselves silly and then head out to another location to drink themselves stupid and then proceed to pass out in a pile of their own vomit or tears.

Thinking that this was too much for me, I decided to head back to my room and call it a night. As I made the trek back to my dorm, I decided that the best idea would be to place one foot over the other as if walking a sobriety line; this was to make sure that anyone whom I came into contact with would know that I wasn't drunk. Despite being the path I took everyday, it takes me 20 minutes to get back to the room—walking like a penguin with two left feet and getting lost along the way. Once in my room, I lay down, and quickly resolve that the the night is indeed young and decide to bother my friend next door.

I knocked on my friend's door and told her and her roommate that it was "Friends" night, and that we were going to watch the show in my room. They look at me from their beds in a state of confusion, when I then, spontaneously, proceed to lift up and carry one of them into my room. While this was happening, my neighbor came out to see what the noise was about. 'The night is young! Party in my room: let's go!' I exclaimed to her startled face. She reluctantly agreed and the four of us crowded on the bed and turned on the TV.

At this point, I am beginning to feel tired so I lie down, and for whatever reason, embrace my friends leg; although puzzled, she doesn't think much of it and continues chatting with the others and watching the screen. I get up and grab the can of rum and coke to take another sip when I notice the eyes of my friends glaring back at me. Finally realizing that I had been drinking, they decide that the best thing for me would be to get some sleep.

I wake up the next morning feeling like I had been hit by a bus, my head spinning, my body aching. I feel as if I have done something wrong, I feel like I have let myself down, that I have gone against the things which I stand for.

I feel sick

Lost

***

As I looked around my room I saw my TV sitting on the nightstand, innocently staring back at me with its big black eye; I saw my PlayStation inviting me to indulge in a couple hours' worth of mind-numbing screen watching; I saw the clothes in my closet reminding me of the consumer culture that I had bought into; I saw my reflection in the mirror.

Overweight
Under slept
Under lived

At that moment, I knew I had to change. I could feel that I was not leading the life I was meant to lead.

I stared at the young man in the mirror looking back at me. I saw his sad eyes displaying the expression of a dog in a cage. I saw the infinitesimal fire burning ever so slightly in his heart—just trying to show its radiance. I saw frustration manifesting, like a sickness spreading throughout his whole being.

I saw a man waiting to be reborn.

That morning, I decided to go for a walk. Despite the blistering cold, I was determined to make it to the riverbank. I think I was also yearning to feel, to really feel what it is like to live.

I made it outside and begin laughing
I laughed at the insane cold that existed in October
I laughed at the revelation I had that morning

I laughed at the fact that I was walking in the freezing
cold before the sun came out
But the sun came out
Like it always does

I smiled at its return

I now realized the truth: I realized that the night of
drinking was just a learning experience, a chance for
me to know emphatically that I love to be in control of
my body and mind—that I wish to live cleanly.

God, it felt good to be alive that morning!

***

The second week of autumn
The air is cool
The distant breath of winter
The scent of fallen leaves
Carried by the gentle wind
Kisses your cheek
Introducing you to the other side of summer
The beauty of impermanence
The reliability of change

I had this ritual during my first semester at college where after my first couple of classes I would get lunch, bring it back to my room and eat in peace with some relaxing music. This would be coupled with a cup of pumpkin spice coffee, open window, a welcoming breeze and some work on an essay that needed completion.

The cup of coffee perfectly accentuated this ideal afternoon.

I realized that after my revelation, I was beginning to see the habits and ideas in my life that were not serving me, the habits and ideas that were not taking me closer to my goals.

But then I realized
Wait a minute
I don't have any goals!

I thought about this problem for a while. The goals I

had, I questioned their authority. I questioned whether they were truly *my* goals, the things that I wanted to accomplish in life, or if they were goals that I *thought* I needed to have, goals that society, or my parents, had lined up for me. I made a resolution to stop what I was doing, to arrest my current situation and work toward uncovering my own goals.

So, I began with what was in front of me—I started with the coffee. I noticed that as the weeks progressed, the one cup afternoon ritual was quickly turning into a two cup and then a three cup afternoon tradition—I made a plan to get it back to one cup. I enjoyed the taste and didn't want to eliminate this pleasure from my life entirely, but, at the same time, I did not want to become addicted and reliant on a beverage for my happiness and wellbeing.

The same idea went for food. I decided that I would experiment with reducing my meat consumption (which was a lot easier than I thought) and then work to find alternate foods to fill the vacuum. My dinners at night went from mystery meat products, some overcooked vegetables, cola, and ice cream to tuna fish sandwiches, salads, pizza, and water.

Not healthy by a long shot, but I was feeling better and on the right track.

I began noticing a transformation in my body and mind and wanted to experiment further. Over the coming weeks, I would work to eliminate all meat products from my life, most eggs, about half the dairy, and most processed foods like potato chips and candy.

It was funny: the more fruits and vegetables I ate, the better I felt.

Go figure…

MOMENTUM

*'It is the mark of an educated mind to be able to entertain
a thought without accepting it.'*
Aristotle

That summer, I decided to consume as much
information regarding food as possible: nutrition, diet,
anatomy, biology, dietetics, etc. I spent my days outside
reading countless books and my nights watching
documentaries on the various subjects. I quickly
discovered that I had been lied to, that *we* have been
lied to. All that we commonly know about protein,
calcium, sugar, diabetes, fat, disease, cancer, meat, and
dairy has been a gross misconception of reality.

Determined to make a change in my life, I decided to
follow all of the enlightening information I had
obtained and experiment with a plant-based diet. A
plant-based diet eliminates the consumption of meat,
dairy, eggs and fish, and replaces them with an
abundance of whole, unprocessed vegetables and
fruits.

I'll be honest, it was difficult in the beginning trying to
go without cheese and other dairy foods.

There were times when I would be invited over
someone's home for dinner, and, despite knowing my
current diet experiment, they would craft a dish
containing cheese or milk.

What was I supposed to do; not eat what they had prepared for me?

I was finding it difficult to overcome situations like these, inconveniences that made it difficult to follow a plant-based diet. I would also come to learn that cheese contains naturally occurring opiates and that when we consume it we don't realize that it is physically addictive. Once I learned this, I decided that I didn't want to be a slave to any one, let alone some food group! I chose to forgo cheese and other dairy from that moment onward on my quest for health—my experiment with what I would later know as veganism.

On this journey of better health and well-being I have come across two main reasons why people don't follow, or at least attempt a plant-based diet. Despite the conclusive evidence that a plant-based diet works wonders to heal the body of many ailments and reverse all sorts of diseases including heart disease and diabetes—it is still regarded as a fringe idea, something only the most desperate of health cases undertake.

It has been proven that humans across the earth can thrive eating this way. Whether you are 5 years old or 95 years young, it is a sustainable lifestyle that can be practiced throughout the course of your life. Indeed, humanity has been eating this way since the dawn of civilization. We do not have to look far to see examples of plant-based diets fueling healthy cultures all over the world. From ancient Rome to traditional China, many of these populations have derived the majority of their sustenance from various types of vegetables and grains, such as, rice, potatoes, barley and wheat. For example, the gladiators of ancient Rome ate so much barley that they were known as the "Hordearii" or "Barley men."

This is not to say that these societies did not consume meat: on the contrary, they most certainly ate meat and other animal foods, but not in nearly the abundant quantities that we find ourselves eating today.

So we know that it is a time-tested lifestyle, but the question remains: why do we continue to eat these rich foods in quantities that cause us to die prematurely and live out the later half of our lives in discomfort and sickness?

The main reasons are situational inconvenience and societal condemnation.

***

You have been invited to go out with your friends after work to a restaurant that you have never been to before. Having no time to even think about your decision or look up a menu, you decide that you want to spend time with your friends and that surpasses your wanting to change your diet. You get to the restaurant and lo and behold, no plant-based options! You look at the menu, thinking to yourself 'great, what am I going to get now? There is nothing here and I'm sick of just getting a salad; plus I know that won't even fill me up!'

As you contemplate the menu with hunger gnawing at you, the waiter comes by asking if everyone is set to order. You look up, from your conundrum with the menu, and see that all of your friends are nodding and handing their menus to the waiter. You start to get red in the face as you clutch onto the menu with more vigor as if trying to transform it into something vegan-friendly. You try to buy time, thinking of what to get, feeling the pangs of hunger settling in, feeling the judgment of your friends piercing your ego.

One of your friends says, "Oh damn, I completely forgot you were a vegan, I'm so sorry!" As she begins to explain to the waiter what a vegan is, you begin to get even more red with embarrassment. Just wanting to fit in, you finally say, 'No, no it's alright, I'll just have the cheeseburger.'

Sound familiar?

This is just a small example of the two aspects that keep us from following our convictions, even when it's something seemingly unremarkable as experimenting with a plant-based diet.

***

The problem is that this modern world is set up to make us weak—mentally, spiritually and physically.

It is extremely easy to go a mile up most roads in suburban and urban America and get some greasy, fast foodlike-substance (to call it food would be a bastardization of the word entirely), while it is difficult to find fresh organic fruits and vegetables or restaurants that serve high quality meals crafted with nutrient-dense ingredients. Guided by the corporate food industry, our communities have these borderline addictive and disease cultivating foodlike-substances foisted upon them, instead of health promoting foods which would create a healthier and happier populace.

Despite these circumstances, I always say that if you want something in life you will make it happen; if you don't want something in life you will make excuses.

'Most of the shadows of this life are caused by standing in one's own sunshine.'
Ralph Waldo Emerson

THE FORGOTTEN

*'The worst sin toward our fellow creatures is not to hate
them, but to be indifferent to them:
that's the essence of inhumanity.'*

George Bernard Shaw

The forgotten
Those that go unnoticed
Out of sight
Out of mind

According to the USDA, in 2008 over 18 billion
animals were killed for consumption in the United
States—when I first read this, I nearly fell off my chair.

How is it that we consume that much meat as a nation?
While this number is now old, it still paints the
necessary portrait of the fate imposed on countless
creatures. According to Dr. John McDougall M.D., over
a billion people worldwide are overweight and have
hypertension, 312 million of those people are clinically
obese, 197 million are diabetic and 18 million die each
year from heart disease.[1]

Could there be a correlation between meat
consumption and our health?

I became obsessed with the question of eating animals.
I asked myself, 'Do we need to eat the flesh of another

species, or can we maintain vigor and vitality without consuming these foods?' Surely we need meat in some respect to sustain us, otherwise why would we consume so much of it? I was confident that the lives of these animals were not lived in vain, that their lives could be fulfilling and given a beautiful and gracious end.

Or so I thought.

As I investigated, information surfaced that pointed to the conclusion that this immense production and insatiable consumption of animal products is both unnecessary and unhealthy, and that there is no biological imperative that would incline us to eat animals.

We can probably agree that humans should not be regularly subjected to, nor threatened by violence, that we should be free to live our lives whichever way we want, as long as it does not harm others, or impede on the freedoms of the group. Do animals have an innate right to live free lives as well?

If we truly care for the well-being of animals, shouldn't we put action behind our words and free them from servitude? Slavery is treating a person as property and forcing them to work: animals are forced to produce a product, whether it be milk or their flesh; be it man or beast, bondage is bondage.

I agreed that animals should not be treated as inanimate property, but felt that perhaps our actions were justifiable due to our survival. In any case, shouldn't we at least think about what our consumption is doing to our health and the health of the various natural systems that sustain us?

As a nation (and increasingly a world), we are consuming more resources than the earth can keep up with, at a faster rate than its renewable essence can replenish. I am well aware that despite the excessive nature of the current paradigms of civilization, the planet will continue to be, whether covered in vast expanses of plastic bags or an incredible diversity of flora and fauna. However, we may not be able to adapt to the changing conditions before it's too late.

Our world may be in need of saving, but *the* world is not in need of saving: it will continue to exist whether we exist or not.

This is a problem: we are perpetuating a system of destruction, one which goes against the laws of nature, that benefits a small minority while continuing to be a detriment to the majority.

I search for what I can do to be a part of the solution rather than the problem.

***

Is there a legitimate reason to consume animals? In his book *The Starch Solution*, Dr. John McDougall M.D. addresses how animal-based foods are harmful to our health and cause all sorts of issues in the body, and that they should generally be avoided:

'What I witness every day are serious diseases that stem from eating animal foods, including heart attack, stroke, type 2 diabetes, arthritis, osteoporosis, and cancer. It doesn't matter whether those foods were processed by a large corporation using additives and chemicals, sold directly by a trusted organic farmer, or raised in your own backyard. All animal foods cause illness when consumed in amounts typically found in a Western diet. Why? Primarily because they are the wrong foods for humans.'[2]

So, if we are not eating animals out of nutritional necessity, why do we continue to consume them and their products? If we know the effects they are having on our health, why do we persist?

I became obsessed with searching for answers; I found no credible evidence that eating meat was essential.

I could only find evidence supporting the fact that many of the animals that we eat are far more intelligent than we are told. For example, pigs are known to be very similar to dogs (in terms of their behavior). They are known to have a wide range of emotion and are communal animals that form complex social groups.

Why do we have pet dogs but not pet pigs? Why do we (in America) eat pigs and not dogs? Why are we forcing such complex and intelligent creatures into a life of servitude just for the indulgence of taste? Are these brief pleasures worth the price?

While the intrinsic value of these animals needs to be acknowledged, I also believe that it is critically important to maintain the various distinct cultures that enliven the world's true diversity. It is possible to maintain their integrity, their rituals, without the added animal misery.

I felt nauseous, starting to see the hypocrisy of my life and the way I viewed food and our food choices as a nation. If we say that we love animals, that we love this world in which we call our home, then let us prove it with our deeds—courtesy and simple compassion demand no less.

***

I wondered why we continue to eat meat and other animal foods in America despite the vast amount of data that shows that even a minimal intake of animal-based foods is injurious to the human body. I wondered why, in this modern age, people would still take their kids to eat at McDonald's and other fast food establishments. I wondered why, as a country, we would continue to deceive ourselves when we buy chicken at the market and justify the act by declaring that it's a "lean protein" without fully understanding the consequences of our purchase. What these examples all have in common is that they are coated in dogmatic thinking. Dogma is the problem here. More accurately, it is the blind following of dogma.

As a people, we choose to ignore logic, science, truth. We run blindly toward the future with the bells of dogma ringing in our ears. We are not headed toward the future; we are headed toward the past with the mindset that ignorance is bliss, that there is no need to question, let alone *change,* our way of thinking.

Instead of complaining, of focusing on all of the things that are "wrong," I started to work on my own life, and began to examine the ideas, habits and beliefs that I was holding onto just because it was "what you do" or "it's how things work" or "it's what you are." In the past, I would have taken in these beliefs hook line and sinker, but in questioning them, I became unfettered from the confines of my restricting viewpoint.

That which binds us—that which holds us—is the key

to our salvation—to our redemption.

Once I started questioning the dogma of the place I grew up—suburban America—I began to see the pitfalls and shortcomings of this way of perceiving the world. The pseudo traditions that have been passed down were keeping me from realizing the rawness of reality and experiencing my naked truth. I was able to look at my own beliefs from an outside perspective, from an objective point of view, and see what were my own thoughts and what were those of others whose beliefs I blindly accepted as truth. Having a critical lens on the outside world allowed me to have a critical eye toward the inside.

Ideology can be a dangerous beast
Without reflection
It can cloud the clearest of minds
Devour common sense with ease
Rush over reason in a giant wave
"It's how things are" is its mantra
"It's the best we can do" is its prayer

Its prevalence throughout the ages
Is testament to its power
Time alone does not heal all wounds
Action does

Question your beliefs
Retire from those which do not reflect your inner truth
Leave them in the grave

Create your own thoughts
Embrace your own creed
Stay sovereign.

***

Animals embrace the totality of their nature
Communicate their intention directly
But we're different
So we think

In our efforts to remain cordial and civil
We withhold truth because of existing social protocols
We fear being "politically incorrect"
Or being ostracized by the community
We apply learned behaviors from those around us
To effectively self-censor our every thought and action

Having the courage to speak our mind
Embracing our inner truth
We embrace our nature
We embrace our humanity
Regain our dignity and honor

The foundation of a peaceful existence is intention, honesty, compassion, mindfulness, and understanding.

A shift in consciousness and awareness that emphasizes mutual respect between humans and all other life forms which share this ecosystem, is connected to respect and cooperation between all human cultures throughout this world.

It became clear to me. I refuse to be a hypocrite in the face of my own virtues, for it is a man's duty to fight for his sovereignty and the ideals which he holds dear to his heart.

Ignorance is bliss
But, in ignorance, we cannot see.

'The man of courage thinks not of himself. Help the oppressed and put thy trust in God.'
Friedrich Schiller

LET IT BURN

'What you do speaks so loudly that I cannot hear what you say.'
Ralph Waldo Emerson

'You burnt the money!' Luke exclaimed with a smile.

After a minute of quiet contemplation, he added, 'You let it burn, for better or for worse—there's no going back now.'

I looked at my friend in a state of confusion, thinking to myself, 'What could he possibly mean by "burning the money"?' After nearly three hours of enticing conversation, I was beginning to feel the unforgiving call of sleep and was not ready to take on yet another of our interesting dialogues.

Seeing the puzzlement and weariness on my face, he explained, 'You know that guy who decided to go to Alaska to live in the wild—he burnt his cash and social security card, cut up his license and buried whatever was left in his wallet and hitchhiked his way to the Alaskan wilderness.' He said without a breath, and concluded with, 'You're just like him, you burnt the money and all other means of turning back—there's no returning to the life that could have been.'

I smiled, not only at his bravado and succinct ability to discern exactly what was on his mind, but also for the feeling that his metaphor gave me. I felt a sense of bliss

at the realization of my ability to follow my heart's
convictions no matter what anyone else does or says.

He then reminded me of the story of the young man
who decided to leave his established life, his place in
society, for an adventure into the wild. The man's name
was Christopher McCandless, and he would go on to
inspire many (including myself) throughout the United
States to question the path they are on and to search for
the meaning of their individual existence. McCandless
decided that the domestic life of a college graduate was
not for him, and that the path which he was currently
on felt disingenuous; he did not know what the answer
was, but was sure that he needed to take action—he
needed a radical departure.

So in the summer of 1990, he decided to take a chance
and leave his life behind, everything he has ever
known, to travel the country on his way to Alaska. At
one point in the early stages of his travels, his car was
disabled in a flash flood and he decided to take off the
license plate, bury it, and continue on foot. His journey
is portrayed in the book, and film, titled *Into the Wild*. It
was at this point that he decided to burn what is left of
his cash, his social security card and whatever else that
would tie him to his former identity.

No going back

McCandless's story would leave an imprint on my
impressionable 14 year old mind that would carry
through to the present day and be a part of my
subconscious. Around the same time that I was reading
about McCandless, I was learning about the various
challenges facing the human species.

I remember learning about the amount of pollution and its effects on the water, air, soil, plants and animals—how various chemicals have seeped their way into the support systems that make life possible and are harming our bodies without our awareness. I also remember learning that nearly half the world's population lives off of less than $3 a day; that millions of people die from malnutrition worldwide despite the abundance of food on the planet.

Is this really what "progress" looks like?

The more I learned, the more I questioned. I wondered why our nations are falling apart and why we continue to act as if everything is alright. I wondered why so many of us decide to neglect the grave reality of our situation despite its severity and need for our mindful and urgent action.

I wondered where the sacred warrior class has gone—the natural defensemen of all that we hold dear.

As a collective, we seem to loathe what were once revered as virtues by our ancestors. We, in turn, revere those traits that they held to be vices—practices and behaviors which bring grave detriment to the tribe. I wondered how we went from proud, beautiful, vigorous, and righteous people, whom honor such virtues as truth, honesty, faithfulness, integrity, strength, courage and kinship; to timid, frail, and weak-minded folk who have discarded the sword of self-defense, and willingly taken upon the chains of pacifist submission.

I was beginning to see through the various illusions that

are put in front of us, creating a hologram of normalcy. It seemed as though the deeper I examined the various sectors of our current paradigm, the clearer the problem became.

I became conflicted by two opposing paths: On one hand, I saw the light of primordial truth in all its rawness and the genuine freedom which it enables, and was drawn to its magnanimous brilliance. On the other hand, I saw various material comforts and sedatives covering life's grim realities, and, despite their faux existence, its seductive fragrance was luring me further and further down its destitute path. I was falling deep into a coma—a nightmare masquerading as a dream.

I reached a point where I needed to make a choice, I needed to choose which path I was going to travel with the complete understanding that there was no going back.

Overwhelmed
Feeling impotent and guilty
I became apathetic
Shrinking deeper and deeper into desolation

Throughout high school and then university, I grew accustomed to these facts and figures about the world and grew increasingly apathetic and uninspired, because I felt the problems were too big for me to face. I thought, 'How could I possibly make any sort of meaningful change as one individual when these issues seem too big to comprehend?'

Each of us has a responsibility to one another and the environment which sustains us; it is a matter of duty and being conscious of your circumstances—making choices that align with your own virtues and vision for the future. I decided that no matter how small the action may seem, it was my responsibility to take action in the face of these problems.

I took my power back.

I took responsibility for the world around me, and began to see the various circumstances that our populace was facing not as some sort of problem or burden that was placed upon us, but as a challenge. It is an opportunity to transform the deterioration and degradation around us—to create something beautiful, something infinitely more sustainable, that is more akin to the wise old ways of our ancestors, than with the great degeneracy of the modern world today.

So, thinking of Emerson, and the idea that our actions are worth infinitely more than what we say, I decided to live my words and put to praxis what were merely ideas.

I chose a path
Forward
No going back

The countless "what ifs" and worries do not matter
It is more important to take action
To walk the walk
My actions in harmony with my words
To not only speak the change I wish to see
To embody the change I wish to see

***

For there to be a better world, we must first examine our own lives. We must first begin to ask ourselves the tough questions and confront the demons that such questions might stir to the surface. So, I started with myself: started to look at the habits, opinions, and dogma that I had acquired throughout the years, and began to experiment with alternatives.

Life experiments

These experiments have helped me to discern what is sustainable in my life versus what is contributing not only to my detriment but to the detriment of the greater environment of which I am a part of; It became a quest to combat the technocratic, materialistic and suicidal anti-culture we find ourselves currently living in. The more I examined my life and conducted various life experiments, the more I was able to realize the power I had in having an impact on this world. In doing this, I chose to permanently abandon the path most traveled today—the path of comfortable compliance.

Let it burn.

RETURN YOUR REVOLT INTO **VIRTUE**

.III.
PRAXIS

THE SIMPLIFYING CHALLENGE

'I went to the woods because I wished to live deliberately,
to front only the essential facts of life, and see if I could
not learn what it had to teach, and not, when I came to
die, discover that I had not lived.'

Henry David Thoreau

I remember sitting in English class one afternoon in high school—it was 10th grade and I was feeling on top of the world. The teacher wrote the above quotation on the blackboard. For some reason, it clicked with me—I understood what this Thoreau guy was saying! This was my first exposure to Thoreau, a man that would influence my life more than any other historical figure.

Fast forward five years, and I am sitting in a class in university titled "Eco-criticism" and we are beginning to read Thoreau's *Walden*. I am delighted remembering the quotation on the board in high school, immediately enraptured in Thoreau's poignant prose and elegant outlook on simplicity.

Simplicity—this word seems to be the cornerstone of Thoreau's life and has burrowed its way into my psyche, leading me on a path of hacking away at the inessentials in my life.

I knew while reading Thoreau's *Walden* that I needed to make some changes in my life. I wasn't sure how. All I knew was the life I had created was becoming foreign to me. I had outgrown various ideas, habits, and hobbies and was ready for a radical departure. I came up with 'The Two Week Simplifying Challenge.'

I decided to emulate Henry David Thoreau. I wanted to live deliberately and, like Thoreau, I wanted to live as simple a life as my responsibilities as a student would allow. This experiment was not in any way designed to be a replica of Thoreau's experiment at Walden Pond, but merely inspired by it. Thoreau spent a period of two years in the woods living in his one-room cabin and living off the land. I chose to take the essence of what Thoreau was trying to convey in *Walden*; simplifying our life, focusing on the things that matter, returning to nature for guidance and inspiration. I wanted to live without the distractions of technology— the Internet and media—to retreat into my own thoughts and examine them for what they are, to be constantly present, in the moment, willing to take life strictly for what it is. As the two weeks unfolded, I dug deeper into my own mind and found out what truly makes me happy. What ensued was a wonderful and meditative adventure *through the eyes of Thoreau*.

Rules

The premise is to cleanse my body and mind through the elimination of excess "dust:" simplifying my life in all aspects, what I eat, what I do, and how I go about my days. I wish to learn to live with less—to experience bliss in the simple pleasures of life.

No cell phone use

Cell phone will be in airplane mode (not sending or receiving any signal) for 2 weeks, only to be used for filming videos. Document each day with a video, talking about the experiment and my experiences with it

Limited Internet and computer use

No news, social-networking, or any other websites. Use computer only for email, and writing assignments. —exceptions include any work related internet links

Limited electronics use

No watching or listening to TV, radio or music, or playing video games—exceptions being links in emails or walking by and accidentally listening

Limited media exposure

No reading news, watching news, listening to news or talking about news

Limited car use

Using car once a week. Use biking or walking as main source of transportation

Simplified Diet

Plant-based diet: 80% or more calories coming from raw fruits and/or vegetables, 20% or less coming from cooked vegetables and starches such as rice, potatoes, etc. No oil or vegetable fat. Little to no salt intake (no added salt). Simply eat until full—no calorie restriction or overindulgence. Start the day with 1 liter of water and drink at least 3 liters of water each day. No drugs, i.e. caffeine, alcohol, etc.

Access to outdoors

Must be outside at least 2 hours each day. Work on garden at least 2 hours each week.

Exercise

Exercise at least 30 minutes each day. Walking, hiking, running, cycling, pushups, etc.

Reflection time

Devote each morning and evening to journal. Read a random excerpt from *Walden* each morning and embrace those ideas for the day. Write a poem right before lights out. Listen to the sounds of the day.

Rest and sleep

In bed by 9:30 most nights. Wake up to the sun. Listen to the body when it communicates and react appropriately (i.e. tired, foot hurts, headache, etc). Consciously move at a slower, more mindful pace.

Entertainment

Entertainment only through other people, including, conversations, lectures, books, plays, etc. Walk in nature at least twice a week.

Theory vs Practice

It is important not only to talk the talk, but to walk the walk as well. I noticed that when spending time with friends or having dinner with family, we would inevitably talk about how we as a society and as a people have to be more conscious of our surroundings, of what we consume, and of how we go about our days. For the longest time, these conversations didn't faze me: I thought, 'Well yeah, things are quite dystopic here, people should be more conscious of their decisions!'

Wait a second.

Why am I thinking about what others "should" be doing while I continue in tacit complicity with that which I find detestable? Do we ever stop to think about effectively applying the theories and ideals which we speak about in our own lives? How can we expect others to follow a path of true sustainability when we, the people advocating for a sustainable future, fail to make the necessary changes in our own lives? With this experiment, I wanted to stop this hypocritical way of thinking and instead take action and let the actions speak on my behalf.

If I fail to apply these theories and ideals in my own life, what gives me the right to tell others how to act or feel, or what to do? It is just as important, if not more important, to live our own life sustainably than it is to preach or teach sustainability; people only learn by the examples set forth by others. We all have the power to make changes in our own lives, whether these changes be profound and inspiring, or just mundane and ordinary, it is a choice we must make; for every every action has its consequence.

For this experiment, I wanted to put these ideas and concepts to the test and make my own life an example of sustainability, an alternative to the mindless materialism of the modern world.

Taking time for the things that matter:

Vigor

Passion

Tradition

Meditation

Mindfulness

Riding a bicycle

Living purposefully

Teaching self-reliance

Cultivating robustness

Having new experiences

Wandering & discovering

Aimless afternoons in nature

Embracing and cultivating community

Less time with television and more time in conversation

Eavesdropping on the blue jays in the trees

Being present in the moment

Developing relationships

Philosophical musings

Studying the cosmos

Refining new skills

Eating "slow" food

Breathing deeply

Industriousness

Hospitality

Humility

Fidelity

Honor

This experiment would become a response to the current social conditions in which I found myself living. I was in a world which did not seem to value things that I felt were critical to a healthy and meaningful human existence.

I recorded my experiences and feelings during the two weeks in my journal. This was a way for me to get down my thoughts and also what Thoreau did— keeping detailed records of not only his musings but also his work in the field and on the house. Here is one of the daily journal entries I made during the two weeks. It details what time I woke up and went to sleep, what and how much I ate and drank, and how much I exercised. I wrote down the thoughts I had that day as well as a poem before I would lie down to sleep.

Excerpt from my journal:

7 April 2013 Day 4: Two-Week Simplifying Challenge

Wake Up: 8:20am

Food: 7 banana smoothie, bowl of fruit salad, 2 liters of water, 2 bowls of rice and beans

Exercise: 2 hours gardening, 2 hours running

I think of how beautiful the silence is, the silence of the wind. How it carries with it all the troubles of the world —blowing, howling, and whisking them away.

Last semester I had the feeling (while working/watching *Robeson*) that I wanted to be on stage, and I said to myself I was going to audition—that never happened. Watching *Dog Sees God*, I am making a promise to myself that I am going to audition for Deb's show next semester, no matter what.

Imagining how easy it must be for most people to just give up and give in to that life of quiet desperation. I feel it is hard, extremely difficult, to fight this and really work on yourself and your values. This reflection time is opening up my mind to what is important.

While writing, I find myself wanting to check Facebook
and other sites; I realize all of this stuff is just a
distraction from letting the mind work its way through
and rediscover what truly matters.

I want to reduce the clutter in my life further. I will go
through my old clothes I no longer wear and give them
away. Why do I need 6 different color dress shirts
when I only wear one or two? Same idea with pants.
Reduce the quantity and use things until they are no
longer repairable or functional.

This Pencil

Thousands of words and commas

Hundreds of faithful days

And it is still here

Functioning

Serving

They tell me I need another one

I say this one is perfectly good

It does the job

It writes just as well as ever

The eraser is fading

So is its color

But it writes on

The idea is simple

Beauty

Utility

Reverence

The simple man's trinity

Lights out: 8:45pm

***

For two weeks I kept a record of what I ate, when I slept, how much I exercised, how much time I had outside and my overall experience during the challenge. Looking at the "awake" times as well as the "lights out" times, I saw a pattern developing, where I would always get up around the same time (average 6:25am) and go to bed within a similar range (average 8:13pm). There is something inherently meditative in this practice of recording your daily activities; I soon found my mind heading toward solace.

There were a couple of days during the experiment when I was outside for at least 7 hours: these were, undoubtedly, the best days of the challenge. There were also days when I would "break the fast"—as I called it. These included watching videos, spending too much time on emails, Skyping twice, and accidentally listening to a CD in the car. I would always feel let down when these happened, as if I had cheated or failed in some way; but I quickly moved past this way of thinking and got back into the process. I found great pleasure in keeping this simple way of life, and great displeasure when moving away from the simplicity and back into my old habits of cluttered thinking and hasty movements. I was beginning to see a path in my life develop which I wanted to explore more.

Eating Simply

During his two-year adventure, Thoreau chose to eat a simple diet: he refrained from luxuries such as coffee, meat and tea, and instead, opted for foods that were for pure sustenance. Thoreau saw the inherent inefficiency of eating animal-based foods, and chose to adhere to a diet predominated by what he grew and what he could gather wild in the fields. I too, chose to live on a simple array of foods; plant foods such as potatoes, carrots, and kale. By eating mostly fruits and vegetables, in their raw state, I wanted to try to recreate that same sense of simplicity of diet Thoreau would have encountered. I imagine he did not use the stove or fire often for cooking and merely ate food as it ripened.

'I learned from my two years' experience that it would cost incredibly little trouble to obtain one's necessary food, even in this latitude; that a man may use as simple a diet as the animals, and yet retain health and strength ... Yet men have come to such a pass that they frequently starve, not for the want of necessaries, but for want of luxuries.'[3]

Thoreau knew that for the human body to get all the nourishment it needs, we need only to eat what nature provides in abundance, i.e. Plant-based foods. Through conducting his experiment on his own body he was able to determine this truth in his life; instead of listening to the opinion of others, Thoreau chose to heed the wisdom of his own nature from that point onward. In simplifying my own diet, I found a sense of peace.

I used to be concerned with making elaborate and fanciful dishes that would provide new tastes and sensations. I would go out to restaurants for the novelty of trying new foods with different tastes and textures: now I recognize food's purpose as sustenance and such experiences don't enliven as they once did.

While I recognize and appreciate the beauty of the culinary arts, my desire to seek excitement from my food dwindled as my desire to find a greater truth increased. I now eat to replenish the fuel that drives me to live a purposeful and intrepid lifestyle.

I eat to live rather than live to eat.

By simplifying your diet you become more aware of your body; becoming more aware of your body enables you to become more aware of the world around you, seized by the moment, happy and adopting a philosophy of gratitude. It begins with the food, what we choose to put into our bodies. Once we clean up the way we eat, the harmful things we put into our bodies, we can move onto addressing the other areas of our lives that need consideration; but without this foundation of nutrition we cannot begin to work on these other facets of existence.

***

'I am no more lonely than a single mullein or dandelion in a pasture, or a bean leaf, or sorrel, or a horse-fly, or a humble bee ... Why should I feel lonely? Is not our planet in the Milky Way?'

Henry David Thoreau

Thoreau not only simplified his diet, but all aspects of his existence, including his social life; he understood the importance of being in the company of oneself as well as being in the company of others. With his Walden experiment, he was interested in delving into his own mind, to experience life in the woods and its uninhibited richness.

I can be alone, but I can be far from lonely—there is a great difference between the two. With the birds singing, the squirrels leaping from branch to branch, the trees swaying and the wind howling, I am not lonely, not in the slightest, for I am in the best company. On the other hand, I could be lonely surrounded by other people. If I am at a social event with those whom I share nothing in common, with whom I do not resonate, I will undoubtedly be lonely.

Some call me a loner because of this. Fine: I accept the label. I would rather be a loner and feel the rawness of this life—feel part of the vast nexus of existence, with all its richness and grandeur, than be surrounded by those to whom I don't relate, and partake in superficial conversations, relationships, and activities. Thoreau shared this idea that it is impossible for us to be lonely when immersed in solitude: we only need to look outside ourselves and experience the true beauty that lies in the wondrous world we reside in, our vast Universe to which we are inextricably linked.

This is partly why I embarked on this experiment: I wanted to see how I would feel if I took away superficial interactions and relationships and cultivated meaningful connections and experiences in their stead.

The Effects of Less Technology

I felt liberated once I let go of various unnecessary uses of technology. I refrained from cell phone use, Internet, movies, television, music, etc, and was able to focus more on self-growth and development, which led to activities that directly benefited my goals. I was writing more, reading more, exercising more, and focusing on cultivating meaningful and worthwhile relationships with people whom I care about.

Without the constant distraction of the cellphone sounding off with a phone call, email, text message, or tweet, I was free to do whatever I wanted to without the constant interjections by the needy supercomputer master in my pocket. Even the simple act of meeting with someone was more enjoyable and worthwhile, because if we planned to meet somewhere, it was my duty to get there on time, since I had no cell phone to tell them if I was running late or wouldn't be able to show up. It made the experience more engaging and active, but most importantly, it made it *intentional*.

Like all of my actions for those two weeks, I made it a responsibility to make my actions deliberate and deeply rooted in the moment. This led to a worthwhile set of experiences where, by leaving myself open to change, different doors would open up and I would, like water, flow with the current.

I found myself sensitive to and more aware of the
amount of technology in our lives, from the countless
people on the bus who are on their phones, to those
walking and texting on a beautiful afternoon, and the
insane amount of televisions blasting around the
university campus. I became frustrated at first, because
I wanted to be in a quiet environment without all of
these outside pressures and distractions. It was hard to
escape. But once I realized that they, too, were a part
of being in the moment, I was able to reflect on the
situation and see it as an opportunity for growth.

Throughout this experience, I couldn't help but think
about David Orr and his exploration of this love of
nature vs. the engineered love of "progress" and the
allegiance to technocracy. In his book *Earth in Mind,*
he addresses this issue in terms of "Biophilia" and
"Biophobia" and what it means to have a sustainable
society. Biophilia is defined as intense love of and
devotion to all aspects of nature, the feeling that there
is an innate bond between humans and all other living
systems. Biophobia is fear or antipathy toward all other
living things and natural order. Orr argues that it has
become more important than ever for us to move away
from this destructive way of living. He posits that the
time has come for us to move to a sustainable and sane
practice of everyday life that incorporates the values of
Biophilia:

'A sane civilization that loved more fully and
intelligibly would have more parks and fewer shopping
malls; more small farms and fewer agri-businesses;
more prosperous small towns and smaller cities; more
solar collectors and fewer strip mines; more bicycle
trails and fewer freeways; more trains and fewer cars;
more celebration and less hurry; more property owners
and fewer millionaires and billionaires; more readers
and fewer television watchers; more shopkeepers and
fewer multinational corporations; more teachers and
fewer lawyers; more wilderness and fewer landfills;
more wild animals and fewer pets. Utopia? No! In our
present circumstances this is the only realistic course
imaginable. We have tried utopia and can no longer
afford it.'[4]

I wondered how I could live consciously in a
seemingly unconscious world. So I "went into the
woods": I went into the woods of my own mind and
tried to detach myself from society and my established
customs and convictions as much as I could in order to
ascertain how to live in society and do the work
necessary to initiate significant change.

Implementation of Theory

Halfway through this challenge, I realized that what I was doing was part of the grand reworking of this modern world—a revival of virtue—a return to virtue. It is a revolt against the destructive, artificial, and nihilist path of materialism we have been following, and into the realm of reason.

A primordial traditionalism.

By simply practicing a theory, listening to the primordial voice of reason inside, we are exhibiting the greatest gift we can give back to our community: you don't have to cure a disease, or invent a solution to combat world hunger, you only need to start with the self.

In other words, by embodying my virtues, my mere existence created a ripple effect in the lives of those around me. Professor and philosopher Timothy Morton would agree with this way of thinking, this proactive and bottom-up approach to ecology and sustainable living. In his book *The Ecological Thought*, Morton argues that it is imperative that we not only become honest with our current global situation, but that we become radically honest with ourselves and habits in this world.

'Thinking the ecological thought is difficult: it involves becoming open, radically open—open forever, without the possibility of closing again ... This is what *praxis* means—action that is thoughtful and thought that is active. Aristotle asserted that the highest form of praxis was contemplation. We should not be afraid to withdraw and reflect.'[5]

Mindful thoughts and actions are the heart of the Simplifying Challenge. It is one thing to discuss the changes needed nationwide , but it is entirely different to practice a theory in our own life. Being radically open means being ready to address the problems that lay beneath the surface within us: we cannot be afraid to embrace these challenges that may come from directing our intention inward.

Embrace the warrior spirit

This challenge was an exploration into simplifying all aspects of my life, as well as delving into the mind to better understand my perception of the world. It was a humbling experience which allowed room for a greater truth to reveal itself. After the two weeks, I have a greater appreciation for life in its simplest form. I don't *need* to be stimulated by superficialities such as frivolous television programs or fear-inducing news; I can sit in the sun for an afternoon with or without a book and be contented.

Thoreau went into the woods for two years, created his own shelter, cultivated his own food, had minimal possessions and minimal interaction with society, embraced the little things in his life; and worked to understand his place in the vast network of American society as he knew it during the 19th century. I, on the other hand, went into the wilderness of the mind for two weeks; broke down the shelter of my ego and my possessions; chose to eat simply and for sustenance alone; used only a handful of possessions throughout my days (journal, pencil, *Walden*, laptop, water bottle, 2 books, watch, etc.). I had no interaction with news, media, television, music or movies; nothing that would distract my mind from being present and in the rawness of each individual moment. I, too, embraced the little things in my life, and ventured to find my passion and purpose in this world.

***

'I had three chairs in my house; one for solitude, two for friendship, three for society.'

Henry David Thoreau

As Thoreau recognized, it is important to reintegrate yourself into society after time spent alone and in solitude; he understood the urgency of not only retreating into the solace of your own mind, but also of working with the brethren of your community for the betterment and preservation of your common folk. It is one thing to go "off the grid" and become self-sufficient on the outskirts of society, but what good does this do for your fellow man? In my experience, after this two-week challenge I now understand why Thoreau went back into society; he understood that to make any sort of change in the world, you must be part of it—you must engage. I could have easily ventured further into solitude, but what benefit would that bring to the community? What greater good would come of that?

Upon my re-entry to the world, I talked to as many people as possible about my experiences during the experiment. They were generally intrigued, and curious as to why someone would do something so drastic. A conversation would then ensue about unmindful consumption, finding ones passion and generally living a more intentional life. After our conversation, most people would walk away feeling inspired themselves and with a new sense of vitality—all of this just from a brief interaction. How could I have had such influences without sewing myself back into the fabric of society? It is our duty to give back to a world that has given us everything—it has given us life.

Finding that balance between living minimally in solitude and being in society interacting with others is critically important to ones ability to make the greatest impact possible. By remaining steadfast to the will of your heart and dusting off your mind—ridding it of those thoughts that no longer serve the best intentions, your distinct talents and passions are able to breathe and subsequently reveal themselves in all their splendor.

Thoreau puts it plainly: if you follow your dreams, your heart, you will undoubtedly find success. Thoreau's experiment at Walden pond and my Simplifying Challenge are testament to the power of seclusion and reflection. It is apparent that most of us living in this modern age can benefit from such an experiment. Right here, right now, while you are reading this, you can begin an experiment of your own. Your own Simplifying Challenge. By reducing the physical and mental clutter in your life, and simplifying the mechanics of everyday existence, you can start ridding your mind of that which may be holding you back from experiencing the true satisfaction and fulfillment that you desire. By heeding the primordial wisdom inside, you choose the high road—the path of Spartan simplicity. The choice is yours.

THE STUFF EXPERIMENT
The Theory of Impermanence
|||
The Practice of Non-Attachment

'Simplicity is the ultimate sophistication.'
Leonardo da Vinci

Coming home one day, I walked into my bedroom with all of my familiar things around me, things that I have obtained over the years. I sat at my cluttered desk and opened up my computer. I proceeded to surf the Internet, not having any particular destination.

This was my habit
Day in
Day out

I was reading an article on minimalism and how these two men changed their lives from a corporate consumerist lifestyle to an intentional and meaningful one—with less stuff. They did this by looking at their possessions and asking themselves if the things in their lives were making them happier. All of a sudden, I found myself looking at all of the stuff in my room, the things I was surrounded by.

Why do I have all of these decorations on the walls?
Do I need five jackets?
Nine pairs of shoes?
Why am I holding onto yearbooks from middle school?

I found myself asking many questions but not having any answers. The truth is that I didn't know why I had so many things that I simply did not use or need.

Have I become a hoarder?

Fearing that I was losing my sanity, I challenged myself with one question: what if I broke these habits of accumulating and consuming, these habits which I have formed over the last 20 years? This question got me excited: the potential was enough to spur me into action. I was embarking on a new experiment!

After doing some research into minimalism, I stumbled upon the idea of having a "packing party." This is where you pack up everything that you own into boxes. So I did just this: on March 1st 2014, I invited a good friend over to help pack up my life. We packed up everything I owned, from my desk to bed sheets, in an effort to discover what it was that was essential and what was just unnecessary baggage hindering my evolution.

What I was left with was an empty room and a giant pile of boxes. The rules were that when I needed something I would simply take it out of the box and after using it I would put it back where it belonged; for example, if I took out a shirt, I would use it and then hang it in my closet. The goal was that at the end of the month I would see how many things remained untouched in the boxes; if I didn't touch something for a whole month, was it really that important to me to begin with?

This, of course, includes exceptions such as winter jackets, snow boots and other seasonal items; I would not be using these items during the month, but would inevitably put them to use once the appropriate season rolled around.

At the same time that I was carrying out this experiment, I decided that every day for the month of March I would give away at least one significant item, albeit a shirt, book or some old shoes I was holding on to "just in case."

Thus the Stuff Experiment was born!

***

Observing how people all over the world react to natural disasters and other extreme events, I started to ask myself: what if I were in that situation, would I react as positively as them? Would I be as resilient and irrepressible as some of these individuals are? Take those who live in Japan, for example: their culture and history centers around this idea of impermanence and change.

'The list of Japan's seismic events dates back to the year 684. Japanese ideas about religion, architecture, theatre, and literature are based on *wa* and *shunyata*—concepts of plentitude and uncertainty, of togetherness framed by impermanence.'[6]

The ideas of impermanence, and its twin, non-attachment, are fascinating to me. I understood them intellectually, but wondered if I understood them on a visceral level; I decided that the best way I could experience this theory of impermanence was to practice non-attachment. I asked myself the question: what am I willing to walk away from?

As a kid, I always admired characters in stories that were determined, focused and able to distill their lives down to the simplest components; I was fascinated by the lore of simplicity that these characters conveyed and found that I gravitated to those with the ability to refine the essence of their life.

Living effectively and mindfully

I try to live my life this way. I call it my backpack theory. Whether it is an idea, relationship, habit, or material possession, I make sure that it fits into my physical or metaphorical backpack. If something doesn't fit, if it is too cumbersome, if it restricts my movement, then I let it go. What's the point in attaching myself to anything in a world that is by its very nature impermanent? Spartan simplicity.

Spartan simplicity: Reducing your thoughts, words and deeds to their utmost essential nature and forgoing that which is frivolous and ineffectual to your goals—a distilled rawness of life. It is living by a creed, a code of honor; having loyalty to something greater, something beyond mere flesh and blood.

I understand that some may dismiss this notion and label it as insensitive or cold. But I disagree: I believe this to be the highest form of understanding that one could embody, for surely clinging to something in a desperate manner in a world where impermanence is law is certainly to be regarded as unrealistic and illogical.

If I acquire a new item, for example, I have to make sure that I don't allow myself to get too attached to it; I have to make sure I don't assign too much significance to it and allow my identity to be tied in with it. This means going with the flow and not being attached to the idea of having or not having "it"—to merely let things come and go as they do. This simply means that I won't allow myself to be dominated by the things I own. By adopting this "backpack theory," more opportunities arise in my life, because I am simply more flexible; I become more adaptable to whatever situations emerge.

OK, look, I know that I'm only in my 20s, without a spouse, children or a mortgage and you might be thinking, 'What does he know?'

You're right: I don't know anything about those obligations, but what I do know is that once we allow our lives to be dictated by the *things* in our lives, or when we allow ourselves to be pulled around by our relationships, we have lost all of our power—forfeited our freedom. We surrender ourselves to external forces and we have a relationship dependent on certain conditions, which is no relationship at all, but an obligatory constraint; which, of course, is detrimental to all parties involved.

***

I am advocating examining the things in our lives, both physical and non-physical and questioning whether or not they are serving us. For instance, when I went to Hawaii for 36 days I wanted to bring everything that I could possibly need—I didn't want to be caught off guard in any situation.

So I brought the following:
8 pairs of underwear
6 pairs of socks
2 pairs of jeans
3 pairs of shorts
2 pairs of swimming trunks
Rain jacket
3 button up shirts
6 T-shirts
Sandals
Hiking boots
Running shoes
Umbrella
3 books
My journal

This does not count all the electronic items, food, "survival equipment" like waterproof matches, emergency blanket, compass, etc. (I don't know who I was kidding), as well as other knick knacks. I threw everything into a 70 liter backpack and packed it to the brim! Not only this, but I also had a smaller 32 liter backpack that I used as a carry-on which contained such "necessities" as my laptop, camera, books, and iPods (yes for some reason I thought having more than one was necessary). I quickly realized how absurd it was lugging around all of these things as if there were no other shops left on the planet to supply me with what I may need on my journey. I ended up trading in the 70L and just using the 32L for my subsequent trips, as well as giving one of my iPods to a friend.

She was going on a trip to Europe and didn't have one, so I told her, 'You know you're going to need this more than me.' She looked stunned: 'Really? Wow, thanks. I'll give it back as soon as I return.' I told her there was no need: if she didn't want it anymore, she should give it to someone else who might find use from it. She still looked stunned, but reluctantly agreed and thanked me.

I learned that giving is the highest achievement we can make as people, and as Thoreau once said, 'Goodness is the only investment that never fails.' It is said that, as humans, we operate on a higher echelon when we are happy, compassionate, and giving to others. That's not surprising given the fact that when we are angry or frustrated at a certain situation, we lack the mental clarity needed to deal with the circumstance at hand and often regret our reaction after we have "cooled down."

We know that people who have giving attitudes give more of their time, more of their wealth, more of their heart and soul to others are, in turn, met with more than they could imagine. This is not surprising once we realize that giving is just the other side of receiving.

What you sow becomes your harvest.

***

This principle of cause and effect applies to ideas and habits as well. If I come across and accept a new idea or a new habit into my life I do so because I know it has the potential to add merit. The ideas and practices of today shape the life I live tomorrow. It is an investment that I am careful to pursue, because I know of the consequences that will emerge from it.

Over time, my ideas evolve, adapt, improve, and change; as new information becomes available I need to be willing to accept the newly acquired knowledge and allow my ideas to adapt accordingly. As new information comes in, my perspective grows and becomes more sophisticated. The same applies to any habit or routine I find myself in: if it no longer serves my highest intentions, then I drop it—I let it go.

There cannot be growth without decay.

This willingness to renounce my pre-conceived ideas and habits means that I am prepared to grow, to continuously pursue a better version of myself without the worry of carrying the dogma of yesteryear.

To move with Spartan vigor.

This creed also applies to relationships, for if I decide to pursue a relationship I know that I must be worthy of the love of my partner, and that it is not an automatic guarantee; I expect that she, too, will be applying the same principles. By communicating and remaining aware of each other's unique needs, we build trust and a truly meaningful and sustainable relationship. This strengthens the bond between ourselves and others, for we recognize our highest potential and hold ourselves (and our loved ones) to it.

By having this self-assurance and fidelity, we avoid being attached to someone through a selfish insecurity. This "love" is insincere, often sprouts out of our own frailty and self-doubt, and should not be mistaken for authentic adoration. The point is to realize these insecurities that we may bear before we throw them unwittingly into our relationships.

When we take full responsibility for what we experience in our daily reality, when we realize that the life we experience today is a direct result of choices we made in the past, we move from the destructive victim mentality to a proactive self-actualizing way of life.

Locate the illusory constraints that you may have allowed fester in your mind. These act as viruses in the brain and prevent us from taking the necessary action in our lives. They need to be removed if any change is desired. These limiting beliefs do just that: limit the potential of the beholder and confine them to a prison of the mind. As Socrates famously said, 'The unexamined life is not worth living.'

If you think you know the truth
You don't
Keep digging
Be persistent
Bear courage
Never stop questioning

The Experiment

*'Simplify the problem of life,
distinguish the necessary and the real.
Probe the earth to see where your main roots run.'*
Henry David Thoreau

The following is a list of items I donated or discarded
during the month of March.

1st:
C-wrench
Laptop lock

2nd:
3 video game controllers
4 DVD's

3rd:
15 articles of clothing
2 yearbooks
5 books I wrote as a kid

4th:
2 books
Pair of sneakers
Jacket
Pair of pants

5th:
6 books
Yoga mat

6th:
Set of bamboo utensils

7th:
Sweatshirt
2 pairs of underwear

8th:
Pair of boots

9th:
Pair of sandals

10th:
3 shirts
5 pairs of socks
Winter hat
Handkerchief

11th:
2 jackets
Shirt
Book

12th:
2 books

13th:
N/A

14th:
Desk
Tea kettle

15th:
2 shirts

16th:
Book

17th:
Game console
Sleeping mat
2 video games

18th:
5 keepsake items

19th:
4 yearbooks

20th:
Pair of sandals

21st
Sweatshirt

22nd:
Water bottle & sunglasses

23rd:
3 pairs of socks
4 pairs of underwear
Sweatshirt
Pair of shoes
Belt
3 ties
Hat

24th:
Board game
TV
Headphones

25th:
10 photos
High school diploma
High school cap and gown

26th:
6 keepsake items
3 textbooks

27th:
N/A

28th:
Old love notes
Suit jacket

29th:
2 DVDs
Lamp

30th:
4 shirts

31st:
7 CDs
2 posters
Shelf

Estimated total: 142 items

In doing this experiment, I was not trying to prove any hypothesis or theory: all I knew was that I felt there was too much "stuff" in my life, most of which I probably did not need. I saw a problem and wanted to try out a possible solution. I ended up donating more than half of my wardrobe, getting rid of a television and video games, books, and baggage. What I chose to let go of made me lighter: it made me free to pursue more meaningful things that would make me stronger in both body and spirit.

At the outset, if you would have told me I would be getting rid of most of the things in my life, I would have told you that you were crazy. This experiment has given me the skill of letting go, the ability to find room for what is important. I am now able to discern whether or not something will be of value in my life; I can sense when I am pacifying myself with trivialities or when I am genuinely using a thought, idea, relationship, skill, or hobby to make me a better person—to help me become the man I was destined to be.

I found that holding onto things for whatever reason, be it money, security, nostalgia, or convenience, was holding me back and not allowing me to grow. This is a practice that the elders of many different cultures over millennia have embraced: it is a way of enjoying life, of enjoying the moment.

'In our zazen practice we try to let go of fear. Whatever happens will happen. We are ready for it.'[7]

In the wake of one of the most devastating tsunamis in

Japanese history, many still embrace this philosophy, because they realize there is no point in being attached to any outcome or their fears and worries—they understand impermanence.

Even when he has lost everything, this Japanese tsunami survivor still gives:

'As we stand, Kazuyoshi hands us four fresh tomatoes, just picked from his tiny garden … "This is absurd. You have nothing and you're giving us food," she says. He stares hard at her: "The less I have the happier I am … I lost everything. Now I feel better".'[8]

By practicing non-attachment in this way, we are essentially preparing for death—preparing for that moment when we lose everything material that we have acquired during our lifetime. This is something that most of us have a hard time coming to terms with; however, it is one of the most important things we can learn to do. When we begin to worry about our possessions, whether they will get stolen, broken, damaged, or lost—when so much of our energy goes to the protection of said items—we cease to enjoy them and become a slave to them. If this happens, we no longer own our things: our things own us.

I understand that my experiment does not compare to the realities of many around the world, but I wanted to try to understand, to have gratitude for the things I have: eyes to see the sun, ears to hear the birds, a mouth to taste the wonders of food. Having gratitude for what I have in this moment is the most important thing, for with gratitude comes genuine gratification.

Diving into a new level of awareness I felt lighter—energized. I wanted to investigate more, to find out what this experiment had to offer.

Let Go

'Life belongs to the living, and he who lives must be prepared for changes.'
Johann Wolfgang von Goethe

The universe is impermanent
You either grow or decay
Balance
Everything in equilibrium

All things are complex expressions
Energy continually changing form
One expression to another

An oak tree at the peak of its growing cycle
Full of cells, nutrients—energy
Dies and falls to the forest floor
Decays and nourishes various organisms
Becomes an environment which allows new life to
spring up
The energy from the tree did not disappear
It merely transmuted into another form
Maintaining equilibrium
This cycle allows life to continue
A fundamental process of the Earth

I have learned to let go. Practicing non-attachment has
made me a stronger person; it has allowed me to live

and experience the totality of everything that surrounds me. It was easier getting to this point then I had imagined. When my friend first came over, it was mainly for moral support, because I knew I would be reluctant to get rid of certain things. When she left, I sat on the floor in my empty room and stared at the pile of boxes—my pile of stuff, the physical symbol of the excess in my life and I immediately had the impulse to reduce—to let go.

I started by sifting through the box which contained all of the books I had acquired over the years. Do I still read this? Do I still get value from it? Could someone get more use from this than I am currently getting? The process was surprisingly invigorating, because it allowed the control to fall back into my hands.

Starting anew

When I came upon my yearbooks, I noticed that holding onto them was pointless, and I could not think of any good reason to do so. Do I really need to be reminded about my high school experience when I am 70 years old? I was reluctant to give them away because of the memories tied to them and I liked going back and reliving those memories. I found myself getting swept up in the allure of nostalgia, its scent quickly bringing me away from the present and back into the confines of the past. Realizing I didn't want to live in the past, I decided to get rid of the books.

I made a compromise with my fragile, nostalgic self: I would recycle the books only after I had scanned those pages I found to have value. So I spent a couple hours that night marking the pages that I wanted to hold on to. I came into class the next day holding a bag full of my old yearbooks, ready to scan my memories and secure my nostalgia to prevent it from being lost forever.

After class I spoke with my professor and asked if I could use the scanner in his office. The very act of saying this made me realize how ridiculous the situation was; I realized in this moment that I did not need the yearbooks—they did not define me. The important stuff will always be with me in my mind's eye: no need for a physical reminder. So we walked together and I tossed the books into the first bin we saw. I immediately felt lighter and unencumbered knowing that I was not assigning value to those things any longer—they were no longer a part of my identity.

Embracing impermanence
I move with courage

It takes courage to examine our lives and let go of those objects, ideas and relationships that are holding us back from becoming who we were meant to become. The only sane thing to do in a world that operates in a state of constant change is to follow the theory of impermanence and abide by the practice of non-attachment.

Yield to the laws of nature

By letting go, I now understand that in my years spent
acquiring stuff I had forgotten why I breathe. I had
neglected the simple joy that is existence. Being lighter,
I could appreciate sunsets, the gift of a new day, the
smell of the morning dew. In letting go, I was able to
have time for the things that matter in my life: spending
time helping a stranger with a problem, reading books
that I love. Unencumbered, I have learned the art of
appreciation.

Smiling
My breath
Falling in love
The eternity in a kiss
The sound of the leaves in the wind
The cool earth underneath my bare feet
Sharing a spirited conversation with good friends
The eerie similarities between me and a fly
The infinite complexity of the night sky
The mystery of a campfire
Going to sleep happy
A close embrace
Good friends
Laughing

30 DAYS OF FEAR

*'Whatever you do, you need courage. Whatever course you
decide upon, there is always someone to tell you that you
are wrong. There are always difficulties arising that tempt
you to believe your critics are right.
To map out a course of action and follow it to an end
requires some of the same courage that a soldier needs.
Peace has it's victories, but it takes brave men and women
to win them.'*

Ralph Waldo Emerson

I became fascinated by these challenges, by viscerally
experimenting with my own life, learning and
experiencing things I would normally look past due to
my limiting beliefs and habits—those that are formed
early in life and carried regardless of whether they're
correct or not. In doing this, most of us carry   old
baggage from the past, things that weigh us down and
keep us from realizing our potential. The best thing that
we can do is examine every single thought, habit and
idea that we have built up and carried with us over the
years and see whether or not they are serving us; for
what other purpose do our thoughts have than to serve
us in creating the life and reality that we desire?

So that is why I decided to take part in the 30 Days of
Fear experiment, to directly test and question my own
abilities and see what I am capable of accomplishing
without the encumbrance of fear holding me back. The
rule is simple: each day for 30 days you move toward
your fears. Now, this fear could manifest itself in many

ways, from trying rock climbing for the first time, to finally getting rid of that wedding dress—the face of fear knows many expressions. The purpose is to challenge yourself to reach a potential that would otherwise be hidden under the mask of fear. It forces you to let go of the need to control, and to train the mind to take frequent risks and to go outside established comfort zones.

If something happened during my day that made me uncomfortable, I welcomed it—embracing my fears instead of avoiding them. Just this small change in the way I viewed obstacles revolutionized the way I saw the world and moments of adversity. Instead of moving through life as a victim of my circumstances, I had the ability to see everything that was created in my life as a challenge and an opportunity for growth and learning.

The following details each accomplishment and what fear was overcome that day:

Day 1
Practiced the chest bounce (a trick on the Slackline) that I was afraid of doing.
Initiated a conversation I didn't want to have.
Took my road bike on a woodland trail and hopped a log.

Day 2
Looked every stranger in the eye that I walked past and held eye contact until they saw me, and then smiled and looked away.

Day 3
Donated a bunch of clothes.

Day 4
Rode my longboard down a steep hill, almost falling off.
Despite enjoying the board, I wanted to practice non-attachment, so I gave it to a friend of mine who I knew had a son who would appreciate it.

Day 5
Finished writing the commencement speech for my university's graduation ceremony.

Day 6
Attempted a slackline trick I was fearful of trying.

Day 7
Finally cleaned out my car (after 2 years).
Cleaned up the aftermath of the Stuff Experiment.

Day 8
Graduated from University.

Day 9
Cycled through the library when there was no one around.
Distributed pamphlets into mailboxes.

Day 10
Climbed a light pole and played frisbee from the top.

Day 11
Tried Oil Pulling (a folk remedy where you swish oil in your mouth for ten minutes to help draw toxins from the body).

Day 12
Took my bike up the steepest hill I've ever attempted.

Day 13
Tailored my own shirt.

Day 14
Drove a manual car for the first time.

Day 15
Booked a flight not knowing what the outcome would be once I got there (See chapter titled 'Synchronicity').

Day 16
Went on a bike ride without wearing glasses.

Day 17
Went searching for a group of cyclists to ride with. I
waited by a popular spot and followed them once they
passed by. I eventually caught up with them and joined
their session.

Day 18
Started reading a book and finished reading it that same
day.

Day 19
Took a route to work that I don't normally take and got
lost and was late.

Day 20
Followed every impulse that came to me.

Day 21
Tried to lead a group ride with nine other cyclists.

Day 22
Tried using Binaural Beats to result in a lucid dream.

Day 23
Swam in extremely cold water.

Day 24
In every conversation I attempted to have eye contact
100% of the time.

Day 25
Practiced correct posture all day.

Day 26
Erased all the files on my old computer.

Day 27
Played with a big and sinister looking spider.

Day 28
Sported a mustache for a whole day in public.

Day 29
Took a freezing cold shower for the first time.

Day 30
Confessed feelings I had developed for a scene partner during acting class.

*Also read a total of 6 books throughout the 30 days

Through this process, I was able to overcome the small barriers in my life that were holding me back from experiencing life to its fullest. After accomplishing so much in 30 days, I asked myself, 'Why do I fear certain things?' As I have found out these are just barriers put in place that more often than not cease to reflect the reality of a situation.

If I am fearful of a situation or something, I now notice the fear but am not attached to it. I examine it directly and ask 'what am I afraid of?'

By asking myself this question, I am able to see that most of my so-called fears are merely phantoms of the mind—imaginary ghosts that lack any real substance in the realm of the living.

We can either choose to be a slave to the mind and live in this state of mere existence, or we can have the mind be a servant to us in creating the life we had always dreamed of—a life of limitless potential and ever-expanding wonder.

***

My first century ride was in the summer of 2014. Despite not having trained at all, I accepted my friend's invitation to do the Gold Coast Century ride when he called four days before the event. I always wanted to do a century and this was my golden opportunity. My second thought was that I had not trained properly: I was not strong, or fast enough; I didn't have nearly the endurance to complete the 100 mile ride through the hills of North Shore Long Island. Despite an onslaught of doubt and fear, I decided to go ahead and participate in the ride.

I remember the morning of the ride distinctly; I looked myself in the mirror and swore that I would finish the ride no matter how long it took. If I was about to pass out, or if I only had one leg to pedal with—I was finishing that ride! About halfway through the ride, my courage and determination were tested. At the 52 mile mark I found myself on the ground feeling like I had just been hit by a truck ... wait a minute, I did just get hit by a truck! I was pedaling down the road when all of a sudden a black Suburban made a left turn over a double yellow line and hit me. On the ground, my first thought was whether or not my bike would be able to finish the remaining 50 or so miles to the finish line.

Spoken like a true cyclist.

I managed to hobble my crumpled body and bike to the shoulder of the road and wait for my world to make sense of the situation. It is at this point that I remembered the moment I had with myself in the mirror that morning. I smiled as I thought to myself, 'Well, now you *need* to finish this ride, unless you want to let yourself down.' I chuckled wholeheartedly and remained in good spirits while waiting for the ambulance and police to show up.

The police made sure that I was alright, giving me basic first aid and questioning me on what had happened, and the EMTs arrived to do further medical examinations and tests. All the while, I was surprised at my level of composure, despite a seemingly trying time. I was impressed by my level of poise and my ability to see the situation as an opportunity for growth, as a test to see how much I wanted to complete the ride—I saw it as another Fear Challenge.

A couple of hours passed and I was finally given the go-ahead to continue riding, despite my swelling knee and leg. With a wrapped-up leg and a banged-up bike, I decided that the greatest risk in life is to risk nothing and that I would finish the ride. Two friends were able to work their mechanical magic and get the bike back into a rideable condition. The accident had set us back 2.5 hours and we found ourselves behind the rest of the riders. Ignoring the setback, we hopped back on our saddles and continued on the road toward our goal.

Despite being the hardest thing I have ever done both physically and mentally, I can say that it was entirely worth all the pain endured. The mind is more powerful than we think and whether or not you believe you have made a choice, the mind will follow through and make that choice a reality. Through times of intense adversity lie goldmines of growth, learning, and wisdom that wait for us to rise to the occasion. It is through these times that we see what we are truly made of, for it is easy to be at peace whilst sitting on a beach at dawn surrounded by beautiful scenery, but it takes a true master to be at peace while experiencing deep pain and discomfort. I learned that not only am I capable of more than I think physically, but the fact that I reacted the way I did means that I have come a long way mentally as well.

It is just a choice in the moment: in the moment, we can either become consumed by fear and disengage from the current reality, or we can choose to have courage in the face of adversity.

Living a fulfilling and meaningful life means overcoming those barriers, it means looking fear in the eyes and choosing to operate in the space of intrepid bravery. If you enjoy living in the realm of fear, being led by your fears like a marionette, there is no need for you to change, for what you are experiencing is serving you.

However

If you decide that you no longer want to be a slave to your self-fabricated fear, perhaps this challenge, this book, can aid you in the quest for truth.

You already know what the fear mindset feels like, so why not take a risk? Think of it as your first Fear Challenge.

You have nothing to lose
Everything to gain

'Timid men prefer the calm of despotism to the
tempestuous sea of liberty.'

Thomas Jefferson

WILHELM

Wilhelm is an extraordinary person, the kind of person that brings life wherever he goes, the kind of person that lifts up everyone whom he encounters, the kind of person that radiates warmth in everything that he thinks, says, and acts upon.

I first met Wilhelm when I was slacklining (it's like tightrope walking between two trees) on the campus of Stony Brook University between my classes for the day. It was a beautiful September afternoon and I had been teaching people the basics of how to stand, balance, and walk the line. The line is set up in the heart of campus where most people are located during the day, so you can imagine how many students stop by and look to see why we are balancing on a 2 inch thick piece of woven nylon.

Slacklining is a metaphor for life.

It starts out relatively quiet: I am setting up the line by myself, securing it to one tree and then the other; I share the moment only with the wind. I then begin by hopping on the line, allowing my body to acclimate to the new sensations underneath my bare feet. Once I get comfortable standing, I begin to walk; the stillness of the air around me and the faint sound of the leaves rustling above me—this is meditation. Once I get comfortable with walking, I try out different techniques both familiar and unfamiliar. At this point in time, someone might approach out of curiosity and ask questions and maybe even want to try it for themselves. I gladly accept and proceed to teach them the basics. This draws in others, curious and excited to try out walking the line. I step away and allow them to explore and enjoy the serendipitous nature of the experience, but remain present in case someone seeks guidance.

It is at this moment that I see a man standing further away than most people with a serious look on his face; I think nothing of it and continue teaching the dozen or so people who have decided to join me. As I am holding one person's hand, guiding them while they walk the line, I glance over my shoulder and notice that he is still there, the tall, serious-looking man. I continue teaching the remaining people, listening to their laughter and feeling the energy of the joyful environment. At some point, the group dissipates, and I am alone with my thoughts. I pause to reflect and sit on the line in serene silence with my now familiar friend, the wind. I stretch my arms and get up to get a drink of water from my backpack when I see that the man from before is still standing in the same place. I walk over to him and ask whether he would like to try walking on the slackline. Shaking his head no, he tells me he wants to watch me do it.

So I do it.

I hop onto the line and enjoy the serenity of the moment, the beauty in the realization of the power of now, that all there is and ever will be is now. On the slackline it is easy to remember this, because the only way to stay on the line is to be in the now, to be completely present in the current moment, or else you risk falling. The trick is to always be in this state, every moment of every day, no matter the time or the place, no matter the situation or circumstance; the power of now is an incredible gift, allowing us to tap into hidden treasures. The more we try and escape the present moment, the more we move away from our true nature —the essence of our existence.

All of a sudden, I hear the man tell me that he would like to try, that he is ready. I hop off and watch him take off his shoes and place one foot on the line. He asks me for instruction and I give it to him. He listens intently, as if hearing the most important words in his life. He stands and begins to walk with unwavering focus.

I am shocked at his ease on the line, at his ability to balance effortlessly, but I am most impressed by his expertly maintained level of concentration. I realize that this is someone who has mastered his inner self, someone who has realized the power he has, the same power we all have inside of us, just waiting to be brought to life. He gets off of the line with a beaming smile and immediately gets right back on. I watch him in awe, I can tell that I am in the presence of a master.

He gets off the line and before I can ask him one of the many questions floating in my head, he turns to me and proclaims, 'You are a powerful man.'

I am taken aback and wonder what he means by this statement. I am a powerful man? What could this mean —he doesn't even know me!

Seeing the confusion in my eyes, he tells me that I have a powerful energy and that is what makes me a powerful man. He goes on to explain that the love that I bring to slacklining and my interactions with anyone I meet is a sign of this power.

I never thought of myself as someone with power, let alone a "powerful man." I always imagined myself as an ordinary person, just a regular guy trying to do his best to make a difference in the world and live according to his morals; I never thought of myself as someone extraordinary, as someone who would leave any meaningful impact on the world. But after he said this, after he looked me in the eye and told me not to underestimate my innate power and to cultivate it to the best of my abilities, I began to think twice about the way I saw myself up until that very moment. Could I really be a powerful man? Was I destined to make a meaningful and lasting impact on the world?

It doesn't matter whether or not he was speaking the truth: I welcome this newfound feeling of self-worth, of confidence and I want to know more, so I ask him, 'What is the most important thing in life?'

Unwavering in his gaze, he finally responds with one word. 'Now,' he declares with utmost authority.

'What do you mean by now? Do you mean this specific moment? Are you saying this conversation is the most important thing in life to you?' I ask awkwardly.

Without blinking, he nods and tells me that the moment, the now, is the only thing that exists and will ever exist. He tells me that the secret to happiness, the secret to a fulfilling and enriching existence is the ability to live fully now—to be so enraptured by the moment that you become intoxicated by its richness.

Many say "seize the moment," but I am beginning to realize the truth: that we don't "seize the moment"; the moment seizes us.

I find out his name, Wilhelm, and that he, too, is studying at the university. We continue our conversation as we both delve deeper and deeper into the mystery of life, questioning our very existence. We are both so transfixed by one another and our discussion that it seems like nothing else is happening outside of that conversation.

Finally, he tells me to be wary of my thoughts and my words, telling me that they are more powerful than I think. 'Every thought you have is creative; your thoughts become your reality, so if you want a certain reality you must first think it,' he advises. 'It all begins with thought: you cannot escape it. It follows you wherever you go.'

Live - Fully - Now

***

After our encounter, I wondered what my life would be like if I took full responsibility for every thought I had, if I worked morning till night carefully sculpting the life of my dreams, starting with my thoughts. I figured I had nothing to lose and everything to gain—so I decided that from that moment forward I would continually observe the thoughts that I had throughout the day and record them in my journal at night. I would observe how I reacted to certain people and situations as well as moments where my thoughts manifested themselves into my life as my reality—to my surprise, this happened more often than not. Once I decided to live every decision in my life with courage, I found that the fear I once had disappeared and was replaced with a deep level of sober understanding. I was beginning to see the truth in what Wilhelm had told me that day by the slackline. I was realizing my power.

Each morning I wake to breathe the air anew
To see the new dawn as just that
A *new dawn.*

'The dignity of mankind is in your hands; protect it! It sinks with you! With you it will ascend.'
Friedrich Schiller

.IV.
AWAKENING

SYNCRONICITY

'The meeting of two personalities is like the contact of two chemical substances:
if there is any reaction, both are transformed.'

Carl Gustav Jung

I am sitting in the gutter in the hot California sun talking to a group of oblivious pigeons, 'Why did this happen? Why am I feeling this way?'

Between swigs of what seems like the best pineapple juice ever created, I find the words to speak to these under-appreciated creatures; I decide that these pigeons are the best friends to me at that moment. After copious amounts of tears and conversation between the four of us, I get up and realize the beauty of the situation.

I am in San Diego
Underneath the radiant sun
Happy to be alive

But let's go back: let's go back to where this particular adventure started. It was November 2013 and I was in a play performing as a very physical and eccentric character who is incapable of lying and can only tell the truth; he was so physical that every dress rehearsal I would be ripping my pants, have bloodstains on my shirt, or a tear in my tights. Lucky for me, the costumers backstage would fix any rips, tears, holes, and, evidently, bloodstains. One day after rehearsal I asked my good friend and twin brother in the show if the costumer Claire was seeing anybody at the time.

He froze, turned around and said, very surprised, 'She just asked the same thing about you earlier today!'

I was stunned, but quickly dismissed it as some random coincidence. My belief was that things just happen and that there is no real connectivity to anything.

Man, was I wrong.

***

Claire

Our first kiss was electric, it was as if the whole world stopped in that instant and the only thing that existed was the two of us. We fell for each other and became inseparable. During the show, we became closer and closer until the end of the semester, when she went back home. We decided to see each other during the semester break, so I flew from New York to San Diego, California to stay with her for two weeks.

Each morning was like waking up Christmas morning as a kid. I felt a sense of ease, excitement, peace and jubilation that I didn't think I was capable of feeling. For those two weeks, I was in a state of ecstasy and all was right in the world. After those two weeks, she left to study abroad for the semester and our relationship was left in stasis until she returned five months later. It was difficult losing those intense feelings in such a short span of time, but I knew that we would be reunited soon enough.

The months that followed were not easy by any stretch, but we both made the best of it and took advantage of the unique positions we were in. I was in the midst of my last semester in college, cultivating my vocation and experimenting with new ideas and habits; she was traveling Europe, learning from her environment and discovering her ethos.

We were in two different worlds.

One day in May I had the idea of surprising her once she flew back to San Diego for two weeks. Wanting to rekindle the brilliant flame that was burning in January, I thought this would be a great idea; it turned out her mother did, too. She told me that it was a fantastic idea and that her daughter would love it. This was all I needed: I now had the confidence and the go-ahead from her parents, so I bought the ticket and eagerly awaited our reunion.

Over the next month I planned and crafted the surprise, trying to make it as perfect as possible. I also recruited the help of her mother, who agreed to handle the logistics end of the operation. After we had crafted our elaborate scheme, she told me that there would be a wedding to go to once I arrived and that I would need to bring a suit. I told her no problem, and that any excuse to wear a suit was fine by me.

The night before the flight I laid out everything I would be bringing:

2 pairs of shorts (that were also swim trunks)
Sandals
2 Dress shirts
2 T-shirts
Microfleece
Rain jacket
3 pairs of underwear
Bandana
Vagabonding by Rolf Potts
Still the Mind by Allan Watts
Bamboo spoon
Collapsible bowl
Razor

Shaving cream
Soap
Pen
Pencil
Moleskin notebook
2 Band-Aids
Some packets of sugar
Laptop
iPod
Garmin watch
Wrist watch
Chargers
Headphones
And a black suit

As I packed everything into the 24L backpack I quickly realized that the suit would not fit inside, so I decided to wear the suit on the plane the following morning.

As we touched down in San Diego I had this resurgence of feelings from January. An aspiration that I had been carefully building up these past few months was finally coming to fruition. I felt like the richest man on the planet.

I eagerly made my way toward the arrivals gate as more memories flood by my consciousness:
Seeing her standing there waiting for me back in January
That embrace
I was mad with love
A huge smile filled my face

I bypassed the baggage claim and felt the pleasant feeling of traveling minimally. I made my way to the taxi cabs where they, like dogs sensing your fear, knew I was needing a cab. One man with a radiant and infectious smile motioned with his hand, opened his door and said, 'Please, sir, right this way, I've been waiting for you.'

'I can't argue with that!' I exclaimed to him as I hopped into the cab.

'So, where are you headed boss? No, no, wait a second, don't tell me. Judging by your suit, you either have an important meeting to get to, or you're proposing to some lucky lady' he said with a smile.

I laughed and told him I was headed to the Fish Market by the harbor and that I was surprising my girlfriend there. He then told me about a time he surprised his now ex-girlfriend at her job at this hotel downtown. He wanted to take her on a picnic on the beach so he showed up with wine, a basket, bread, the whole nine yards. Once he got there, she told him that she did not love him anymore and that she had been trying to think of a nice way of letting him know. As he was telling me this story I couldn't help but think of past relationships where this might have happened, and how grateful I was to be in a relationship as sturdy and secure as the one I am in.

I smiled at the thought and asked him how he dealt with the situation. He told me that he got emotional and begged her to reconsider; he asked her why she felt the way she did and what he could do to fix it. He told me one thing that I won't forget.

'I'll tell you one thing boss, don't ever let anyone take control of your life. The moment you give away your control is the moment you lose everything.' He smiled and said, 'It's either that, boss, or you will be pulled around by anyone and everyone you come into contact with.'

I nodded and wondered if I was letting anyone pull me around; if I was living a spineless life.

As I was having this introspective inner dialogue we arrived at the destination, I handed him a twenty and told him to keep the change, aware of and faithful to the concept of generosity. I got out of the cab and cautiously sneaked toward the restaurant, not knowing if she had arrived yet. I sat by the giant statue of a navy officer kissing a woman and admired the various tourists taking pictures in front of it. I let the breeze take any doubts I may have had out to sea and reveled at the magnanimous complexity of nature.

As I admired the beautiful scene, I couldn't help think about the intricacy and grandeur of this elaborate plan we had created. Claire was supposedly meeting the owner of the restaurant (a friend of hers) to talk and catch up. The wait staff knew that I was coming to surprise her and were thoroughly briefed and prepared.

I got up from my seat and started moving anxiously, awaiting the call from her mother giving me the all-clear to go inside. As I paced back and forth, I thought of the uninhibited attitude I had toward risk. From being the kid giving the cutest girl in class the love note, to changing my life path from the comfortable and secure to the uncomfortable and the uncertain, to "burning the money" and not looking back; all of these examples fueled my determination to continue following my heart despite what known or unknown adversities might lie ahead.

At this moment, I burst out laughing at the awesome nature of this journey I was on. I turned to a woman next to me who had been startled by my outburst and exclaimed, 'Wow! Isn't life incredible?' and she just stared at me as if trying to understand what was happening down in the depths of my soul. Eventually, she just laughed and said in a soft and gentle tone something in a language that could have been Chinese. At that moment my phone rang and it was Claire's mother telling me that she had arrived and to go ahead inside. I jumped up in excitement and headed for the main doors to the restaurant. What I didn't realize at the time was that all of those risks that I had taken in the past would seem like nothing compared to what was about to happen.

***

As I enter the restaurant, butterflies swarm in my stomach. I am greeted by the hostess, who takes me to the side and asks in a hushed tone, 'Are you the guy?'

I feel like a spy on some covert mission. I look in the vicinity to see if there is anyone else around who she might be talking to, but once I realize that it must be me, I nod, and she leads me over to a corner of the restaurant that is out of plain sight. She informs me that Claire is on the porch outside and then introduces me to one of the waiters who would be my guide. I am introduced to Ralph, who leads me across the restaurant and through the back door so as to not ruin the surprise and be spotted in advance.

At this point my hands are sweating, my heart pounding with excitement.

I
Feel
Alive

As Ralph leads me to the door, he tells me, 'OK, pal, she's right down there sitting at the end table facing the water … good luck!'

I thank him and shake his hand, immediately self-conscious of my sweaty palm. As I go through the door, I am greeted with the familiar warm breeze off the harbor waters. I turn to my right and see her brown hair waving in the gentle wind.

Time stops.

With a giant smile and an open heart I walk toward her with my arms outstretched. She turns around at what seems like the perfect moment and I put my arms up to the sky and exclaim, 'It's me!'

She looks dazed and confused and is able to mumble out a timid 'H...' before I walk over and give her a big kiss. To my surprise, that electricity, that spark we had from the previous hundreds of embraces we shared in the past is gone. I am so preoccupied with my excitement in seeing her that this fact doesn't faze me one bit. 'She's just extremely surprised, no big deal,' I think.

We sat in silence for a while, as she was seemingly working out the current reality of the situation in her head; this, however, did not bother me in the slightest because I knew how she felt and was confident in our connection. I savored the silence. I enjoyed sitting there in the sun with her, reunited after months of being apart.

I was on top of the world.

After a while, we decided to go for a drive, exploring San Diego.

We visited various beaches, parks and the famous Hotel Del Coronado. As we were driving I noticed that she was still quiet, so I asked her if she had acclimated to the situation yet, she tells me no, and that she doesn't handle surprises well, but she was happy to see me nonetheless.

I wish I had known sooner!

As we continued driving, we made small talk and just enjoyed each other's presence in the small space of her car. We were about an hour away from the city when I noticed tears rolling down her cheeks. I asked her, half-jokingly, if they were tears of joy. She said, 'It feels different. I'm both happy and sad. I don't know why, it just feels different.'

I told her that of course it was going to feel different than it did before, and that's how it works, that's how relationships evolve. After a bit of consolation she turned and gave me a big smile and thanked me for the surprise.

We continued driving for a while, looking at more coastlines, stopping to see different sights. As we were driving on Rt. 101, I turned to her and jokingly asked her again if she had acclimated yet, trying to be funny, referencing her flabbergasted state before. To my surprise, she muttered, 'No,' amidst streaming tears. I was confused, not knowing what happened and asked her to pull over, so she went and parked the car in a lot outside a grocery store. As I tried to comfort her, she continued to cry and tell me that she felt different about me and about our relationship, that she did not feel the same. I tried to ask her what she meant and what specifically she was feeling. She avoided the question. So, I asked whether she wanted me there with her or not. She told me that she did, and that she appreciated me and was grateful for every minute we had together in the past.

I was confused. It seemed as though she was wresting with something, trying to overcome some contradiction in her mind. After about an hour of talking in circles, seemingly not getting anywhere, I reluctantly looked her in the eyes and asked her with confidence, 'Do you still love me?'

After a few seconds, she turned and looked at me with tears in her eyes and muttered, 'No, I don't.'

I am paralyzed.

I asked her if she is certain, 100% sure that she does not love me any longer. She tells me that she is sorry that I came all this way, and for the fact that we are now in this situation. I look down at my arms and legs and realize I am still wearing the suit. I haven't been in California for more than three hours and now I just want to leave and return home.

I feel as though I have been stabbed in the back by my best friend—the person I trusted the most. I feel as though the ground has been instantly pulled from underneath me and I am falling into the center of the earth.

Completely blindsided.

I asked her why all of these feelings were coming up now, and what made now so different than before? She told me that she was just as confused, that she didn't understand why her feelings had changed either.

Given the new reality of the situation, I decide it would be best if we went our separate ways. I told her I would just get a cheap motel room back in San Diego and figure out my plans the following morning; she agreed and offered to take me back to the city.

Thinking that I was going to need food for the night, I hopped out of the car and headed into the grocery store looking for some sort of comfort.

I walked into the air-conditioned building, immediately feeling lost. I stood there, paralyzed. Apparently my body decided to catch up with my feelings and I became stiff. As I stood next to the entrance for what seemed like an eternity, I didn't feel anything, I was stuck in a trance, feeling my world slip through my fingers.

Time stood still.

All of a sudden I regained my awareness and found that I had made my way to the wine section of the store. Realizing that alcohol would only make me feel more isolated, I made my way back to the produce section and snapped out of my daze. I grabbed a loaf of bread, strawberries, and some orange juice and headed over to the cashier. She asked me how my day was going: my reaction was to complain and tell her how terrible my circumstances were. But I stopped myself, because I thought of how grateful I was to be able to feel pain like this, to be able to experience this incredible roller coaster of emotions. So instead of telling her my negative perceptions, I instead decided to embrace the constructive thoughts and tell her, 'I am alive.'

I smiled at her as I grabbed my food and left. As I headed back to the car I was swept up in those unwanted butterflies you get when you know you're in a situation you don't want to be in. My momentary feeling of ease and acceptance was thrown away and replaced with feelings of rejection and isolation. I opened the car door feeling as though I was getting into the car of a stranger. She was in tears after just getting off the phone with her mother, who suggested that we both sleep on it, that in the morning we should go to a cafe and talk things over.

Why would I want to prolong the inevitable? I didn't want to continue feeling this way for another minute, let alone another full day. She informed me that her brother Steve lived in the town neighboring hers and that he would be happy to have me for the night. I declined and told her that there was no point if she was completely certain of her feelings. She told me that she may not be 100% certain and that it would be a good idea to sleep on it and get together the following morning.

On our way back to the city, we stopped for gas and she told me that her mother wanted me to call her. I got out of the car, dialed the phone number and listened to the dial tone while appreciating the man on the corner of the road holding a cardboard sign with 'smile' handwritten on it. I tried to force a smile but probably looked like a nutcase. At this moment her mother picked up and immediately apologized for the situation. I told her that it wasn't her fault, that no one could have predicted it, that she just did what she felt was right. She told me that she was confident that Claire was just extremely surprised and just needed a night to wrap her head around the situation. She told me to trust her and spend the night at Steve's. Despite my reluctance, I decided to take a chance—hell, I'd taken enough chances so far to realize that I had nothing to lose other than a night of restless sleep.

I hung up the phone and noticed that Claire was still filling up the car. I gazed over at the fast-moving traffic of 4:00pm southern California. I saw all the cars speeding in a race to nowhere.

What is so important that we feel we need to move fast, that we need to rush through life in a race to the future —something that physically does not exist? We ignore the beautiful fullness of the present moment. Whether it is radiant pleasure or intense pain, we choose to fly through our emotions, fly through our feelings, in pursuit of this deceptively opportunistic future. The man on the corner with the sign inspires this thought: he seems to be the antithesis of what the traffic represents. This makes me smile, so I decide to head over and talk to him.

I introduce myself, 'Hey, my name is Jayme, I don't mean to bother you but I noticed your sign and it really did make me smile. This may sound strange, but I could really use a hug right now.'

Expecting us to platonically embrace in a moment of true human connectedness, enveloping the bond that ties all of us together in one big human family—I receive the opposite. He declines and simply explains, 'No, I'm sorry, I don't do hugs.'

A lesson to let go of expectations.

Taken aback I ask him why he does not "do hugs." I sit
down and he proceeds to tell me the story of his father
and how he was not hugged by him as a child. He tells
me about how since then he has had a hard time giving
and receiving hugs. I hear a car horn—it's Claire
indicating she is finished. I get up and thank Joseph for
his company. As I turn to leave he says, 'I can give ya a
handshake, though.'

I take his offer, say goodbye, and hop back into the car.
Feeling that familiar sense of uncertainty I choose to
embrace the feeling and just live with it. I choose to
live with my uncomfortable uneasiness and just
embrace the situation for what it is. I choose to stop
feeling sorry for myself. As we drive, she asks what my
decision is: 'Are we heading to my brother's or am I
taking you back to the city?'

I tell her to head over to Steve's apartment.

As we drove, we talked about the situation and how
neither of us saw it coming. I was confident that
everything would work out the way it was supposed to;
of course I wanted things to work out between us, but I
was not tied to that outcome in particular. I was ready
to take a chance and see what hand I was dealt.

As we arrived at Steve's apartment, she told me that he
wouldn't be home until after 6:00 and that I could just
wait outside his apartment on the stairs. She unlocked
the encoded gate which opened up into the small
apartment complex. Before she turned to leave I
reached into my bag and handed her a large bag of
lettuce, swiss chard, carrots, peas and other vegetables
that I had picked earlier that morning from my small

garden back at home. I told her that I wanted her and her family to enjoy it. She smiled and accepted the gift and then turned to go back to her car.

Is this it?

As I stand in a daze watching her car leave, I follow it until it is out of sight.

WHAM! I am instantly hit with what I call my "survival mode"—the imperative need to figure out a plan of action as to how I am going to respond in a given situation. I sit down on the stairs in the hot sun (still wearing the suit) and take out my pad and pencil and begin brainstorming ideas and tactics to make the best of my current situation.

Halfway through my vigorous bout in "survival mode," I realize that it's close to 7:30 and Steve has not arrived yet. I also notice the tenants below me smoking a copious amount of cigarettes, and listening to loud hip-hop music, both of which make me feel irritated and disgruntled, further fueling my desire to execute an effective plan. I glance over at the encoded gate and realize that if I leave I will have to make sure it is the right decision, because I won't be able to return. I decide to stop complaining to myself and instead continue to brainstorm my options.

As I drink the remainder of the orange juice and watch the setting sun, I can't help but think how intense life is if we just open our eyes. Every instant is full of both intricacy and intimacy and we just need to change our perception to see its truth and wisdom. It is at this moment that Steve finally arrives,

'Friggin' girls, man: she may be my sister but she's still a jerk.' He offers his hand in a gesture of compassion.

I shake his hand and tell him what had occurred to lead him to finding me on the stoop of his apartment. He gives some advice and informs me about all of the opportunities that are now open for me. We talk for a while and he offers me an invitation to a big party at his friend's house, I happily decline and offer my thanks for his hospitality.

Once he left, the void appeared and I felt as though I was falling again. My mind was left to freely race around the events of the day. I tried to rationalize everything that had happened and tried to make the best of my current situation—but I couldn't. I kept having that familiar feeling of uneasiness and anxiety; I couldn't sleep, eat, or do anything that night; all I could think about was meeting her at the cafe the next day.

That following morning I woke up around 5:00am and just sat next to the phone like an eager dog waiting for his owner to return home.

The phone rings
It's 9:30
Eager to talk to her, I grab the phone on the first ring.

'Hey! Are you on your way?' My voice practically cracking as I say the words.
'Hey, are you okay, do you need anything?" she says in a cool and calm tone.
'Well, I'm alright, when are we going to meet up? Are you on your way?' I ask in confusion.
'I have nothing to talk about.'

'What? I thought the plan was to talk over coffee, aren't you coming?'
'No, nothing has changed from yesterday.'
'Oh, OK, so you're 100% certain, then?'
'Yes, I'm certain.'
'Alright, well, goodbye then.'
'OK, bye.'
Click

OMEN

*Omen: A phenomenon that is believed to foretell the
future, often signifying the advent of change.*

I instantly erupt in a fit of laughter.

I laugh at absurdity of the situation and the fact that my
monolithic expectations have been severely destroyed
in but an instant. I put my phone in my pocket and start
pacing around the outside of the apartment, taking in
the sun's kind rays while I think. I smile at the familiar
feeling of having to think on my feet.

Sink or swim
Do or die

It's the same feeling I had in England when my cousin
in Germany all of a sudden told me that she bought me
and my friend a bus ticket in Berlin for that coming
Friday—it was Tuesday when she emailed me. So I
quickly got into "survival mode" and found flights for
the coming night and a couch to sleep on in Berlin.
This makes me feel full of life: it is full expression of
what I am capable of.

As I am contemplating my options, I think of how
effective I have been in dealing with the situation and
I'm surprised to be completely at peace with what has
happened. I understand it from her perspective, and

have come to terms with it rather quickly: I am pleasantly surprised. The reality is that I am here for two weeks without a place to stay or any plans whatsoever.

I call my friend Luke out of instinct, because I begin to feel the familiar pull of the amygdala dishing out fear into the rest of my mind, infecting it with its toxic soup. I tell Luke the story and he tells me that this is the opportunity I have been waiting for. 'She decided for you, man. You were on the fence about the longevity of the relationship and weren't sure what to do with your life because she was in it, well, now you know. If this isn't a sign, I don't know what is!'

What he said was true: I had been wrestling with the idea of having a girlfriend who who didn't have the same lifestyle or vision as me. But out of love, and obligation to love, and probably the fear of loss, I held on.

I remember when she had been in Europe only for one month and I had had it; I didn't want to have "dates" on Saturday nights alone in my bedroom with my computer as company. I did not like that our relationship had turned into a series of weekly online communications where I would relay what I had done during the week and she the same. Instead of being a vigorous dance of passion, our relationship was on life support. I was living in the past and holding on to feelings that had come and gone; it felt disingenuous and restrictive. I was ready to drop it, but, in the end, I decided to hang on.

I found myself coming out of my daze, hearing Luke's voice in my ear. 'Home? Why would you go back home? If you go home, you will most likely just stay in the house all day and allow yourself to be upset. Why would you want to do that? Listen to me; if you don't want to be in San Diego, why don't you head up the coast and visit Portland? You always wanted to check it out and, well, now is your chance. So why not just take a chance and go for it?'

I could feel his smile over the phone and I couldn't agree more with his words of wisdom. I made a deal with him that if I could get a flight for the following day to Portland and then a flight from Portland to New York for less money than a flight straight to New York from San Diego, I would make the trip north, up the coast.

I turned on my laptop to check prices and was surprised at what I found.

It was $100 cheaper to make the trip to Portland

I was shocked at this bizarre event—that I could get two flights for less than the price of one. At this point, I got a text message from my father that just read, 'Call Henry' and then a phone number. I thought to myself, 'Who the hell is Henry? And why should I call someone I don't know?"

Trusting my intuition, and my father's judgment, I called the number.

An older man answered the phone and after a few minutes of small talk I finally recognized the voice as my half-uncle who lives on the coast of Oregon. I had

only spoken to him twice before and had no idea what
to expect, but remained open to whatever possibilities
that might arise. I told him the story and he told me that
I could stay with him. I was stunned at his generosity
and told him that I didn't know how long I would stay
for, and that it could possibly be as long as two weeks.

He interrupted me, saying, 'Boy, did you not hear me? I
said you can stay as long as you want. Don't fly into
Portland though, fly into Eugene airport instead; it's
closer to my house.' I smiled at the thought of this great
opportunity to meet my uncle and experience a part of
life that I had never experienced before. However, I
was a little dismayed that I would be flying into Eugene
instead of Portland because I had noticed that the
flights to Eugene were significantly more expensive.

As I was thinking this, Henry interjected, 'Now, I know
it's more expensive to fly to Eugene, but don't worry
about that, I'll pay whatever the difference is on the
two flights.'

Was he reading my mind?

'No no no, I wouldn't want you to do that, thank you
but...' I couldn't even finish the sentence before he
interrupted.

'Did you not hear me, boy, I said I would be happy to
pay the difference. Now quit arguing with your elders
and buy the damn ticket!'

I was learning quickly not to go against his convictions.

'Hey, Henry,' I began, 'Let's have a code word so that we will know who each other is, since we have never seen one another before and I don't know what you look like.'

'Oh, alright, if you insist," his laughter creeping up.

My machismo kicked in: imagining that it would be a large airport and not wanting to get lost, I finally came up with a code word.

'Alright, how about "lemon tree"? If one of us spots the other, we can walk up to them and say "lemon tree" and see if they respond with the same phrase, that way we know we have found each other!'

Slightly confused, Henry agreed, and I thanked him again, hung up the phone, and bought the plane ticket without having a second thought. I was able to see the opportunity through the smoke of my fallen expectations; it had only been two hours since the phone call with Claire, and I had already made plans to leave the next day.

That was fast.

I got back inside and told my exciting news to Steve, his girlfriend and his roommate. They were glad to hear the news and asked what I was going to do once I got to Oregon.

'Well, to be honest, I hadn't thought that far ahead yet' I confessed. 'I'm just excited to be going to the northwest: I have no idea where it will take me.' We continued conversing, and they asked how I was planning on getting back to the San Diego Airport.

"I'm not sure, maybe I can take a train?" I inquire in hesitation. Steve's girlfriend Kate laughed and told me that she was going back home to her apartment in San Diego and that she would gladly give me a ride to wherever I needed to go.

I grabbed my backpack and my suit, and Kate and I hopped into her car. She put on this fantastic music that just seemed like the perfect form of medicine to heal my injured ego. We talked about a variety of things; she told me that she was in the Marines but could not wait to get out and go back to school. She told me she just wanted adventure and to travel the world, where she had no debt, no unnecessary responsibility and nothing to do but live and experience the vast diversity of life.

We connected through music, words and through our kindred spirits. About 10 minutes outside the city she asked where I was headed. I completely forgot to check for hostels before we left on my computer, so I took out my phone and began searching for rooms nearby. 'I don't know yet … let me check some places near the airport and I'll …'

Before I could finish my thought, she told me that she had a spare room and that it was a 20 minute walk from her place to the airport.

I was shocked at how perfectly things were working in my favor: it seemed like the necessary pieces were just falling into place, and the breakup with Claire was the catalyst that set off this new course in my life. Since the seemingly "bad" event that was the breakup, nothing but "good" synchronistic things had been happening. My life seemed to be becoming increasingly optimistic and uplifting as the moments went on.

Once we arrived at her place, my immediate thought was, 'Wow, I need to get a place like this, this is perfect!' The afternoon sun kissed the mahogany flooring and created a warm and rustic atmosphere. I put my bag down on the sofa and began to compliment her on the apartment. She nodded in agreement and began to tell me all the wonderful things about the area, when a 747 jet flew directly overhead. The place shook and I turned, wondering what the noise was.

She erupted in a fit of laughter at my reaction: 'You looked like a scared cat just now! It's just a jetliner, I told you we were close to the airport.'

I chuckled at my not-so-manly reaction to the loud sound and told her that as a thank you for letting me stay, I would like to cook her dinner that evening. She gladly accepted the offer and told me she would be back in time. I thanked her again and we went our separate ways for the day.

I decided to head downtown with my backpack, feeling on top of the world. I passed cars, people, pigeons, all completely oblivious to my state of mind, to this incredible feeling I was experiencing of ecstasy, of completely feeling alive. I wondered what they were feeling as well.

I wondered what the man on the cell phone walking toward me was feeling underneath the exterior, or the woman in the car at the stoplight singing to herself— seemingly without a care in the world.

As I enjoyed the carefree walk downtown I noticed the familiar feeling of hunger so I decided to hop into a grocery store in the outdoor shopping center and picked up two bottles of my favorite juice and some rice and vegetables for dinner. As I walked towards the register, I popped open the top of the pineapple juice and took a couple of swigs.

As I enjoy the juice on the checkout line, I begin to have this feeling rising up from beneath my feet. I feel uneasy, like I am going to fall. I put down my groceries and try to focus on my breathing. I am able to calm myself down. I pay for my things and exit the shop. I begin walking through the outdoor shopping mall, reaching for the juice in my bag; I take a few more swigs and I am immediately swept off my feet. I sit down, not knowing what is happening. I feel a surge of energy rush from the ground, through my feet, up into my head. What is this, what is happening to me? I feel lightheaded and notice that tears just begin to pour out of my eyes. In my pursuit of moving forward, I had been neglecting this vital part of me. I did not realize it at the time but I was inhibiting my body from expressing what it wanted to, what it *needed* to express. I had not yet paid the bill for this experience, and was now about to pay the debt that had been accumulating.

While heading toward the harbor I see a group of
pigeons and decide that I want to be in their company
so I sit down on the curb and began speaking to the
birds. Like some wise group of elders, I trust their
wisdom and proceed to tell them all my woes—my
heartfelt sorrows regarding what had happened. They
come closer, despite my lack of food for them, and I
continue asking them for answers, all the while a
seemingly never-ending amount of tears continuing to
stream down my face.

After what seems like an hour, I notice that the first
bottle of juice is empty, and, all of a sudden, the birds
fly away and my eyes dry up—like the switch was
instantaneously turned off.

I realized that most of us live in a constant state of
sedation. We are brought up in an environment that
teaches us to contain emotions, especially any kind of
sadness or depression, and to control said emotions
with copious amounts of sedatives, be it chemical or
habitual, both act as suppression hindering genuine
expression.

I think about the absurdity of what had just occurred; I
sat down and started talking to a group of pigeons as if
it was completely commonplace. Despite this bizarre
scenario, I continue to make my way to the harbor to
watch the late afternoon sun.

I finally make it to the harbor and snap a picture of the
military ships passing by for my father, who loves
boats. Right after, I get a text message from him.
Coincidence?

'Hey buddy, how you holding up?' It reads.

The now familiar feeling of incredible intensity arises through my body once more. In an effort to guard myself from the pain, I take out the second pineapple juice from my pack—the amber glow is a welcomed distraction from the current moment and I begin to drink a good portion of it.

That's when the floods return.

Just like last time, this unbelievable energy sweeps from the ground, into my feet, through my body and disperses out of my eyes like flowing streams. I wonder why this is happening again, why I am going backwards rather than forwards, I thought I had dealt with these emotions already?

Dealt with ...

Like they are some kind of problem that can be easily solved—a nuisance to be eliminated. I begin to realize my relationship with my emotions, especially those which I had classified as "negative." I begin to just let it go, just let it emerge without judgment, and without analysis of its significance.

For some reason, my initial reaction is to call my father; perhaps I know instinctively that he will know best how to alleviate this heartache. I dial the phone number, despite my inability to catch my breath, let alone to form words in a coherent enough manner to have a conversation.

'Hey bud, how you doing?'

1 Mississippi
2 Mississippi
3 Mississippi
4 Mississippi
5 Mississippi
6 Mississippi
7 Mississippi
8 Mississippi
9 Mississippi
10 Mississippi

It takes me ten whole seconds to gain enough of my composure to muster out a forlorn 'I'm alright,' which was supposed to fool him I guess, despite my obvious state of distress.

After about 20 minutes, my father's final words were, 'lick your wounds and get right back up. You've let out your feelings, you've allowed yourself to grieve, but now you need to allow yourself to live. You're a lot stronger from the situation, now use that strength to your advantage.'

Father to son, his wisdom reigns.

I don't remember my father ever saying anything more meaningful to me than his declaration in that moment. I thanked him and told him that I would keep in touch. I hung up the phone and instantly felt lighter. I felt as if the poltergeist had left my being, as if I had finally exorcized all of my feelings of sorrow from the past and was fully ready to move on. A true learning experience.

As Randy Pausch once said, 'experience is what you get when you didn't get what you wanted.'

I was learning the power of our emotions, how even if we think we are feeling a certain way, our heart might feel otherwise.

That evening I get back to the apartment to find it empty—no Kate in sight. I throw on some music and decide to clean the monstrously large pile of dishes in the sink for her. I feel as though it would alleviate at least one of her worries: to come home to the surprise of a clean kitchen would undoubtedly be a great relief. It was the least I could do for her kind hospitality anyway. Noticing the setting sun, I glance at the clock and see that it is nearly 9:00pm; deciding that she most likely isn't going to make dinner, I decide to cook the meal of rice and vegetables and eat in the company of the cosmos.

That night I sleep like a baby, completely at one with my emotions and in total peace with my circumstances. The next morning I take a walk to the airport, leaving behind nothing but my footprints but bringing with me so much hard-earned experience. I smile, noticing that I have learned more about life in my 24 hours here than I had during my sophomore year at college.

As I board the plane I remember what my dad told me about my uncle: 'He's a redneck, it will definitely be an experience, I'd call it: The Hippie Meets The Redneck,' he laughed.

Not understanding what that meant, I begin to feel slightly apprehensive, allowing doubt to creep back in, wondering if I am making the right choice. I have conjured up this image of "rednecks" in my mind and it isn't pretty.

The Hippie Meets The Redneck

'Be bold and mighty forces will come to your aid.'
Johann Wolfgang von Goethe

I get off the small jet plane, make my way to the arrivals section and notice that there is only one terminal. 'Wow, this is a small airport!' I mutter to myself as I pass maybe ten other people in the corridors of the airport. Leaning on the wall overlooking the parking lot I reminisce on how in the face of doubt and insecurity I have risen above adversity and obstacles, and remained positive throughout.

Well, except for that time with my friends the pigeons.

As I have these thoughts, I slip into that familiar fear mindset. I have never met the man I am about to stay with, I don't know his last name, I'm not sure where I am, I don't know his address, his cell phone number, what he looks like, and whether he is an axe murderer; the only information I have is that his name is Henry, and that our code word is "Lemon Tree."

While I am having these thoughts, and working up an anxious sweat, I notice that there is someone behind me. Before I can turn to see who it is, I hear a rough, sandpapery voice.

'Tinkerbell?'

Confused I turn around to the creator of the voice and
notice that he is around my height (5′ 8″), hardly any
hair on top of his head but sporting a white mullet that
extends down past his neck, his shirt with the sleeves
cut off has a design of four disembodied heads floating
in midair with great big white beards and "God bless
America" written on the bandanas tied around their
heads.

I look up at the man and mutter, 'Lemon Tree?'

'Oh, damn, I forgot,' he says, with a huge smile on his
face.

He gives me a hug and introduces himself as Henry,
and after some chatting, we make our way to his car.
At this point I am excited for this new adventure, the
next chapter in this compelling journey. I hop into his
old Cadillac and we make our way toward the Oregon
coast. We pass beautiful mountains and breathtaking
vistas, and I am reminded at how amazing this world
we share is; how magnificent it is to be living in such a
beautiful time in human history. We make small talk
about my studies, his interests, our family. Our
conversation wanders away from these topics and into
the realm of government, politics, and the
environment. He tells me of his certain philosophies
regarding the cause of the current economic state of
America, and that the government is in shambles
because of a certain group of people. I automatically
begin judging and slapping labels on him instead of
listening to his words and trying to understand his point
of view. Now entrenched in my skewed perception of

him, and the notion that what he is saying is overtly negative and borderline bigoted, I begin to get angry. I challenge what he is saying, and we begin arguing.

I am not even with him for an hour and we are debating things that, for some reason, I feel the need to defend. I feel like he is spreading ignorance and negativity with his ideas and I begin to get frustrated with the situation. I think, 'Wow, this is terrible. I just got here and I already can't stand it! I don't think I can last more than a couple hours with him, we just don't seem to see anything eye to eye.'

I have a familiar feeling of needing to escape, as though I am trapped; I am losing oxygen and being suffocated by the situation. Why can't I seem to get things right? Why do these bad situations come to me? What did I do to deserve to be engulfed in one negative situation after another?

I begin to let the frustration and pessimism sweep through my body and I start to close up. There is nothing for me to learn from being here. If anything, I am going to regress and move backwards from all the progress I have made. I know I have to get out of this situation sooner rather than later, and begin to think of my escape plan.

I begin feeling guilty about the silence that has ensued after our heated argument, as well as my thoughts of leaving. My uncle went out of his way to pick me up from the airport and let me stay at his home, and this is how I repay him?

Not wanting to start off on the wrong foot, I try to steer
the conversation back toward more neutral ground and
ask him what he does for a living.

I need to digress here for a bit, so if you will just stay
with me, this is the truly inconceivable part of the story.

A few days before I left for this journey, a friend of
mine had recommended I read a book called *The
Alchemist* by Paulo Coelho. The book takes place in
16th century Spain and revolves around Santiago, a
young and free-spirited shepherd from Andalusia.
Santiago loves being a shepherd: he loves every aspect
about it, the comfort of traveling wherever he wants,
the relationship he has with his flock and the serenity
of being alone with his thoughts; he has come to be
quite content with his life.

He ends up meeting a young woman whom he falls for,
and is set on marrying her once he has enough to
support the two of them in a life together. Despite all
the great things happening in Santiago's life, he begins
to be troubled by a recurring dream. He has this same
dream every time he visits the ruins of an old church in
the Andalusian hills. Whenever he sleeps underneath
an old sycamore tree that grows out of these ruins, he is
plagued by his dream. In it there is a small child telling
him that there is a great and wonderful treasure for him
at the base of the Pyramids in Egypt. Santiago gets fed
up with the dream and wants to know why it is
plaguing him—he needs answers. He goes into town
one day and consults a gypsy woman. The woman tells
him that he needs to go to Egypt. Thinking that the
woman is crazy, Santiago leaves in frustration and

decides to sit in the town plaza and read his book for a while, to get his mind clear. He is approached by a peculiar old man he has never met before, named Melchizedek, who claims to be the King of Salem. He tells Santiago that he must journey to the Pyramids, that it is his Personal Legend to do so.

Santiago is shocked at hearing the same advice from two total strangers in the same day. The old man convinces Santiago to sell his flock of sheep along with everything else he owns. If he does this, he will have the exact amount of money needed to travel to the Pyramids in Egypt. He tells him to set off for Tangier, the seaport on the coast of Morocco where he can find a caravan that will take him to Egypt.

Santiago takes the old man's advice on faith and decides to follow his Personal Legend. He sells all of his sheep and takes the risk of a lifetime and heads to Tangier. On arriving, he becomes enveloped in the sheer bliss of traveling to a completely new land. The sights are different, the smells are intoxicating, and nothing is familiar. In a bar, not knowing the local language, Santiago manages to procure a friend who volunteers to help him find the caravan to Egypt. His newfound friend ends up robbing him, stealing all of the money he has to his name along with any food he was carrying.

Now angry, scared, and hungry, Santiago just wants to go back to Andalusia and be with his sheep—he has had enough of this Personal Legend nonsense. Just as he is wallowing in his own self-created misery, he notices a shop and admires the glass in the window. He wonders whether he could clean off the glass in the shop window for a hot meal and a place to sleep for the night; he wanders into the shop and does just that.

Santiago ends up spending a year working with the kindhearted and conservative-minded glass merchant, who teaches Santiago many important lessons about life and the importance of following your Personal Legend—something that he wouldn't have seen if he had not taken the risk of staying with the glass merchant. Santiago encourages the merchant in the importance of taking risks, saying that if he were to take even the smallest of risks in his business he would reap major benefits. They both agree to heed the other's advice. The risk pays off for the merchant, and Santiago makes enough money to buy twice as many sheep and have a great home in Andalusia, or just enough money to make it to the Pyramids. The merchant advises him that he already knows the life of the shepherd, but he does not know where the life of the traveler will take him—what life will be like if he follows his Personal Legend.

So what does all of this have to do with me and my situation in Oregon?

While I am in the car with Henry I think about Santiago and what an interesting life he has, how he was able to understand the omens of life and the various signs that seemed to be showing him the path to his Personal Legend. I ask Henry what he does for a living, just wanting to lighten up the mood and stop us both from strangling one another.

As we come to the peak of a large hill the view opens up to the breathtaking sight of the valley below and the view seems to declare that anything is possible.

Henry turns and tells me that although now retired, he used to own a glass shop.

I freeze.

I didn't know how to react, let alone respond to his statement. My mind begins doing backflips, wondering about this unbelievable coincidence. How is it that I had just read this eye-opening book, was just thinking about it, and having this conflict with my uncle, when he tells me at this exact moment that he used to own a glass shop—that, he too, was a glass merchant.

I am shocked: I cannot believe the synchronistic nature of this moment. What are the chances that all of the pieces, all of the various events that needed to occur, would line up to provide this incredibly profound moment in time?

It was at that moment that I followed the voice inside me that said, 'You need to let go of all of your judgments of this man, let go of your own confirmation bias—you obviously have things to learn from him.'

So I did.

At that moment, I dropped everything that I had thought I "figured out" about him and began anew with a completely blank slate. It was as if the reset button had been pushed on the relationship and we had a newfound opportunity to understand one another. So I began to just listen, and I mean really listen. The Buddhists call it "deep listening": a way of listening more through the heart than the ears. It aims at understanding the other person without judgment or criticism; it aims to blur the line between self and other. I wanted to build, rather than burn a bridge between the two of us.

When he would mention something that conflicted with my current bias or cognitive dissonance, I would just ask him a question like, 'why do you feel that way?' or, 'What do you mean by that?' Instead of automatically fighting his opinion, I would simply listen and try my best to understand from his point of view. This practice of listening freed me from the anger and frustration I was feeling just minutes before and granted me a level of empathy that I had never experienced prior to meeting Henry. I truly became interested in everything he had to say and wanted him to share all of his thoughts with me so that I could understand, so that I could share in his joy, his sorrows, and his excitement.

I was beginning to learn that true wisdom often lies in the places which we least expect it to reside. It was incredibly eye-opening and liberating—I had acquired a new ability, "deep listening." I was eager and ready to see how I would grow as a person with this newly acquired power.

Throughout the next two weeks with Henry, I would learn much more about life than I thought was possible. Prior to this experience, I had just been acquiring more and more thoughts and beliefs and piling them onto one another like blocks building a pyramid. I was always trying to be in situations or acquire knowledge that would fit my own confirmation bias—that fit my own precise way of thinking at the time.

Not any longer.

Truth is often hidden in plain sight; it is our own distorted perception of reality that causes us to remain in the dark of our own ignorance. This, of course, perpetuates dogmatic thinking and further keeps us from the light of truth. Only through challenging my own beliefs am I able to travel closer to the sacred wisdom of reality and live a life full of integrity, courage, and veracity.

Question your actions

Is this the kind of man I want to be?
The kind of life I want to lead?
The legacy I wish to leave?

Make a choice
A decision
To be a better man

***

I chose to question my limiting beliefs regarding those whom I saw as "rednecks." While my old thoughts of "rednecks" like my uncle would have been those of disgust, disdain and frustration, I now see not just my uncle, but the world with completely different eyes. I don't see people in terms of labels that our society has put on them, but instead I see the individual for who they truly are—an incredibly complex, and capable human being, someone who has shared in all of the emotions that I have, and is my equal in our shared humanity. This was profound for me, and I would not have been able to learn this lesson had I not taken the risk of staying with Henry.

After a two-week experience with Henry, I left for New York. I will never forget the time we spent together, learning about one another, our shared kinship and the beauty of life's idiosyncrasies. If there is one lesson to take away from the experience, it is to be open to everything and anything life decides to throw at you.

And, of course, the importance of taking risks.

We never know what a risk will bring us—that's the beauty of taking risks and following our intuition. By taking risks and moving outside our established comfort zones, we give ourselves the opportunity to shatter our limiting perspectives about others, about history, and most importantly about ourselves.

The truth cannot be taught: it has to be realized.

I realized that I can create my own reality. My thoughts are creative power and manifest themselves into actions, which then become my reality. I understand now that the breakup with Claire was an opportunity, an omen in my life that signified an opportunity for change.

Nothing more
Nothing less

I understand that it was a chance for me to choose a path, an opportunity to move closer to my own Personal Legend. It became a test, a challenge to see what I was capable of.

You walk on stage, the lights are on you and it is opening night.
Do you follow your gut and perform what you have trained your whole life to do?
Or do you become small, cower, and run off stage because you are afraid?
Afraid you are not good enough
Afraid to fail

The choice is yours

But regardless of what choice you make, you need to take full responsibility for that choice and own it. For it is only when we take full responsibility for our life that we can begin to steer it in the direction we wish to see it go.

So, greet problems in your life with open arms, and see them as challenges. Look your fear in the eye, treat it as the ghost that it truly is; for when you do this, you will notice that the ghost disappears—it loses its power over you. By facing the thing which you fear most, you take away its influence in your life and you become free from its subjugation.

It's time that you risk
Time for you to follow the voice of your heart
The spirit in you
Seeks to experience the richness of life

If your heart is beating
If your lungs are breathing
You owe it to yourself to be alive

You must realize that you are worth it
Whatever seems to be challenging you
Hardship you may be experiencing
Will pass

No one has power over you
You are the master of your own life
The lord of your sovereign soul

I AM ALIVE

'The only person you are destined to become is the person you decide to be.'
Ralph Waldo Emerson

In my 23 years of life, I have learned that only through taking risks, and examining my closest held beliefs and perceptions, am I able to break out of my prison of comfortable sedation and into the life of tempestuous sovereignty.

I had grown weary of the path I was on, the path of attaining an employable degree from a prestigious university, finding a "good" job with security, buying a house, raising a family, and building a career—all the while in an intoxicating trance of consumerism and materialistic degeneracy.

I could feel myself being sucked into a whirlpool and I was becoming restless with the feeling in my gut that I was on the wrong path—that I had become complicit in the degradation of our society and the sacrilegious treatment of the legacy of our ancestors. I knew that I had to make some sort of change in my life, but I was scared. I enjoyed being comfortable in my own discomfort and dissatisfaction, but deep down I knew I was discontented and unfulfilled, and more importantly I felt encumbered, as though I was not in control.

And that's where the experiments come in.

Through conducting the various life experiments, my
mind was freed; I was able to deconstruct the dogma
that I had been carrying for years. I had a new lease on
life—able to realize my potential and carefully and
intentionally craft my life the way I saw fit.

I was hungry
With an intense desire for nourishment
For a sense of satisfaction in my life
To live for something noble

I took action
Took a risk

There are times when I doubt myself
Many nights that I lose confidence
But I remain tenacious
Faithful

Never underestimate the power of winning small
battles
Small victories bring great confidence
Boost your morale
Allowing you to persevere
The courage to fulfill your destiny

Go within or you go without

Seek to know thyself
The truth in you
Awaken

Become
Lead
Master

Greatness beckons!

AFTERWORD

By

Jesse L Liardi

In the pages of this here tome, Jayme lays out his unfolding and yet to be concluded quest for wisdom and experience. It is these two elements; wisdom and experience, that are all-important in the mission for true progress. For progress may be reaped only by wisdom-laden experience and experience-backed wisdom. Jayme has, by his own sheer will and courage, generated his own ethos, worldview, and philosophy, in stark spite of the preexisting notions of progress and spiritual refinement. The conscious effort to experiment with his life as well as to retell pivotal moments from his story illustrate the genuine will that he possesses to aid his fellow man. It is this powerful ability to provide wisdom from his experiences and deploy a tempered, evolving rationale towards future experiences which will benefit the world.

Progress for the planet is decided upon the self-waged progression of all its characters. We cannot expect peace and stability with broken systems and people of broken spirits maintaining and perpetuating said systems. To reach and finally attain progress, it behooves the planet's inhabitants to be honest with themselves and admit where things simply do not work within their communities. As evidence mounts and experience is shared about, for example, the educational system, a community of truly progressive folk may act to correct or perhaps replace such a rigid, spirit-crushing system. If people would at least attempt a small portion of Jayme's challenges, perhaps they would become progressive within the scope of their own lives and thus become part of a greater and global progressive movement for real change in the world. Progress must develop within for it to be upheld in the universe.

By experimenting with the modern unyielding exposure to all kinds of media, Jayme has displayed both the willpower and initiative to understand how both the level of exposure and the content of the aforementioned media affects us all. The piling of possessions has become a sort of de facto cultural requirement, and thus the spartan lifestyle is chastised as delinquent by the great many. His determination to both understand and combat the conventional, technocratic gizmo-laced lifestyle may serve to his contemporaries and future generations alike as an example of how one may transcend such a media-driven existence.

I am very proud of Jayme. As his older brother, I was given the chance to observe his development firsthand. It really comes as no surprise that he has penned such a work and has made such progress. Due to his conscious efforts to utilize his innate wisdom as well as his personal ordeals as confirmed in this book, I can say safely now (as if I could not before!) that he will continue to be an asset to those around him and those yet to be graced with his friendly essence and seemingly boundless savvy. The progress he has made as a person tells me all I need to know about how he will insure peaceful progress to the world.

EPILOGUE

'The two most important days in your life are the day you are born and the day you find out why.'
Mark Twain

While attending university, during my final semester I decided to enter the speech-writing contest to speak at Stony Brook University's graduation ceremony. My speech was written in the spirit of the great environmental writer, Henry David Thoreau, who explains to his readers in *Walden*,

'To be a philosopher is not merely to have subtle thoughts, nor even to found a school, but so to love wisdom as to live according to its dictates, a life of simplicity, independence, magnanimity and trust. It is to solve some of the problems of life, not only theoretically, but practically.'

Taking Thoreau to heart, I decided to write about my experiences during The Stuff Experiment. I was fortunate enough to share my speech with my graduating class in the Sustainability Studies department.

Below is that speech

***

I am conducting an experiment, and I have the honor of asking my fellow graduates, faculty, and esteemed guests for your help. As we leave this place, many of us will be traveling on to new adventures—or just heading back home. What is sure, is that many of us will be packing.

This frames my experiment.

I am going to ask you to visualize all your possessions … all your "stuff" in your dorm room, apartment, childhood bedroom … you get the idea. Now, identify the few things that are most important to you, the few things you absolutely cannot live without. Great, now just hold onto those.

On March first, I packed up all my belongings … from toothbrush to furniture … everything. My friends and parents thought I'd lost my mind. The point of this experiment was to filter through my accumulation of stuff to determine what I actually needed, and what was just superfluous.

Over the next month, if I needed something, I would find it, use it, and not put it back in the box. At the end of the month, I still had a lot of "stuff" in boxes, and I was forced to ask myself, 'Do I need these things, are they making me happier?' You can probably imagine how strange it felt … to have everything I owned and had acquired over the years packed away.

I felt anxious, but I also felt liberated

In doing this experiment, I had no preconceptions and I was not trying to prove any hypothesis. I was not trying to purge myself of all material objects or become a monk. The idea was simply to see from a different perspective, one that could only be revealed through a radical departure.

And so, as we move through life, now and always, I am asking you to take frequent detours from your comfort zones. Letting go is often risky, frequently challenging, sometimes painful, but almost always rewarding.

This is one of the many lessons that I am grateful to have learned at Stony Brook. Other pieces of wisdom that this university taught me are to pay very close attention to process, and the value of dwelling in the uncertainty of *now*. Our future is an experiment, the results of which are yet unknown, and to quote Wendell Berry,

'We don't have a right to ask whether we're going to succeed or not. The only question we have a right to ask is what's the right thing to do?'

We have the choice to live deliberately.

So, my engagement in this experiment is on-going, but as any of you science or engineering grads already know, good experiments require multiple subjects and scenarios, and that brings us back to you and the objects you visualized earlier. As you are deciding what your next steps in life will be, please take just a moment to ask yourself, 'What do I really need to support the future of my dreams?'

Thank you.

'To save all we must risk all.'
Friedrich Schiller

END NOTES

1.McDougall, John A., and Mary A. McDougall. "Our Global Health Crisis." *The Starch Solution*. New York: Rodale, 2012. 70.

2.McDougall, John A., and Mary A. McDougall. "Our Global Health Crisis." *The Starch Solution*. New York: Rodale, 2012. 38.

3. Thoreau, Henry David. *Walden*. New Haven: Yale University Press, 2004. 65.

4. Orr, David W. *Earth in Mind*: *On Education, Environment, and the Human Prospect*. Washington, DC: Island, 1994. 151.
5. Morton, Timothy. *The Ecological Thought*. Cambridge: Harvard University Press, 2010. 8.

6. Ehrlich, Gretel. *Facing the Wave: A Journey in the Wake of the Tsunami*. New York: Pantheon, 2013. 12.

7. Ehrlich, Gretel. *Facing the Wave: A Journey in the Wake of the Tsunami*. New York: Pantheon, 2013. 51.

8. Ehrlich, Gretel. *Facing the Wave: A Journey in the Wake of the Tsunami*. New York: Pantheon, 2013. 24.

38513484R00139

Made in the USA
San Bernardino, CA
07 September 2016